Solo Flight

SOLO FLIGHT

12 Personal Perspectives on the Single Life

Edited by
Jim Towns

Tyndale House
Publishers, Inc.
Wheaton, Illinois

Library of Congress Catalog
Card Number 79-93235
ISBN 0-8423-6052-2
Copyright © 1980 by
James E. Towns. All rights
reserved. First printing
July 1980. Printed in the
United States of America.

This book is presented

in

gratitude to God for his love and grace,

in

appreciation to those who contributed chapters to this volume,

and in honor of the

lordship of Jesus Christ who makes a solo flight meaningful.

CONTENTS

ACKNOWLEDGMENTS

No one ever writes or edits a book alone, whatever the title page may assert. It is not possible that in syllable and in sentence I could adequately express my appreciation for the influence and concern of the many people who have encouraged me in this work.

I am indebted to: 1) Cliff Allbritton, for counsel throughout the writing of the manuscript; 2) Margaret Dunbar, for prayer support; 3) Marilyn McGinnis, for her profound encouragement to me to edit such a volume; and 4) Tyndale House Publishers, for their work in getting this book to you.

Special appreciation is expressed to June Zindler who enthusiastically typed the manuscript.

INTRODUCTION

Sometimes I come in contact with persons who are both deeply spiritual and very real! This book is a product of such encounters. I am a single adult working with singles conferences and seminars. I have come to think that there is a need for a book which would contain perspectives and experiences of singles who have adapted to a life-style of singleness in a couple-oriented society. These writers are some of those people who have consistently put into practice some ideas that the world must hear!

In this book I have gathered together some provocative, interesting, and profound statements about being a single adult. These chapters are broad in scope, penetrating in depth, and straight from the lives of some of the most significant resource people in the area of single adult work. That is another good reason for this book.

The book is a collection of personal experiences and scriptural proclamation. These writers are not preaching at you. They are relating what God has done for them and what he will do for you.

With all the books on the market about single adults, why another? Well, this book is produced in order to extend a ministry of God's Spirit in your life. It is written by people who are adept in dealing with the many challenges of singleness. Each writer is single and is deeply involved in working with single adults. These people have come to understand a deeper meaning to Robert Frost's famous poem "The Road Not Taken," a meaning that has made all the difference. These single writers have traveled an entirely different road from the major segment of society's marrieds.

For many years now nonmarriage has been seen as being abnormal. This viewpoint has changed over the past few years. Writers of the Scriptures did not make an issue as to whether they were single or married. What really made the difference was the message given to the person!

It is our desire that this book will suggest, stimulate, and produce an acceptance of a new perspective toward Christian single adults in contemporary society. Ron Churchill, minister to single adults, begins the book with a scriptural perspective on singleness. Nancy Hardesty, professor of Church History, then deals with the responsibility for singleness. Margaret Dunbar, who teaches in a medical school, gives a professional and scriptural presentation of love, sex, and the single.

In "One Is Not a Lonely Number," there is discussed the distinction between loneliness and aloneness. Sara Frances Anders, sociologist, tells how she is single, sane, and secure. In a stimulating and at times controversial chapter, Steve O'Kelly, pastor to single adults, presents some ideas from his conclusion that there are too many frustrated single adults.

Melva Cook, church program consultant, agrees that problems of those who have never married have been over-dramatized. Len Sehested, homemaker, speaker, and lecturer, seeks to explain the adjustments she encountered as a widow and suggests some helpful hints. Wesley Jackson, religion editor for *The Times-Picayune* in New Orleans, relates the male perspective of losing a mate through death. Cliff Allbritton, editor of *The Christian Single* magazine, profoundly presents the insights of a former minister who is divorced.

Phylis Campbell Dryden, mother-homemaker-provider, gives

deep insights into the pilgrimage of the single parent. Finally, David Ring, evangelist, presents his journey from cripple to conqueror as a physically handicapped single adult.

You have in your hands the statements of successfully adjusted singles in our society. We would want you to know that each of us has journeyed a trail of tears through personal adjustment that produced the peace and abundance we now know! We desire that our thoughts, feelings, and insights will expand your perspective, illuminate your spirit, and deepen your love for people as well as strengthen your commitment to Jesus Christ as Savior and Lord of life!

Jim Towns, Ph.D.
Department of Communication
Stephen F. Austin State University
Nacogdoches, Texas

Dr. Ron Churchill
Minister to Single Adults
Northway Baptist Church
Dallas, Texas

A SCRIPTURAL PERSPECTIVE ON SINGLENESS

There are many ideas mentioned in this chapter that I have never heard from any pulpit in our land. I never learned them at a pastor's conference, associational meeting, state convention, or evangelistic conference. I suppose the rationale is that at most of these meetings, as well as in most of our churches, we are led by married men. With this acknowledgment, and assuming that most people relate best to people like themselves, it is understandable that married men do not advocate or even describe that which is foreign to their recent experience —namely, singleness.

The Bible, however, says a great deal and also implies a great deal about singleness. The more I have studied the Bible, both in seminary and in graduate school, the more I have noticed that its pages are filled with single adults. Jeremiah, interestingly enough, was commanded by God *not* to marry (Jeremiah 16:1-4). John the Baptist, Jesus, Paul, and Barnabas were all single. Of the twelve Apostles only Peter is said to be married (Mark 1:30, 1 Corinthians 9:5). Mary and Martha and Lazarus were single as well as Mary Magdalene, the one that our Lord appeared to first after his resurrection. We do not know exactly when Joseph died, but when he did it left Mary the mother of our Lord a single adult. Luke tells us about the widow Anna, a prophetess (Luke 2:36-38), and Paul mentions Philip the evangelist and his four virgin daughters who preached (Acts 21:9).

As single persons read and reflect upon these verses and these people, I believe the depression that some have over being single ought to be somewhat alleviated. If one does not like being single, the individual needs to do something about it. The idea of sitting at home and praying that God will cause a man or woman to have car trouble in front of your home, that they will not only stop there, but also come to your door, knock, meet you, and fall in love is ludicrous. I believe anyone can get married; it is just a question of whether or not you want to marry any of those that would marry you.

Frankly, I think it is a sin for singles to have that "down-in-the-mouth" negative attitude about their life circumstance. We have a terrible witness for our Lord if we are always unhappy and griping about the state in which we find ourselves. And after all, it is a state which we have chosen and continue to choose daily. Many singles that want to marry are living life in a "holding pattern." There are feelings of self-destruction and self-pity that emerge and hinder development toward what the singles would want for themselves as well as for their Lord.

Singles should assume that they will always be single. If they can accept this assumption, singles can mature as single people and see that single adulthood can be a pleasant pilgrimage. If the single person does marry at a later date, matrimony is a wonderful surprise. If matrimony does not come about, the single does not have to live the continued agony of hoping for that which never happens.

Increasing numbers of singles are learning to say with Paul, "I have learned to be content in whatever the circumstances" (Philippians 4:11, NIV). No one who is single lives in perfect bliss all of the time. But of course, neither do any that are married. Every circumstance has its advantages and disadvantages. What we make of our life circumstance is what is important.

There are some very interesting passages in the Bible about singleness. Because I am one of the very few Southern Baptist ministers who are single, these passages have had a particular interest to me. (By the way, it has always seemed strange to me that Catholic priests could not marry, and Baptist preachers had to!) First Corinthians 7 and Matthew 19:10-12 are focal passages related to this issue. In the Corinthian passage, verses 7 and 8 not only list singleness as an option, but Paul gives it preferred status.

For I would that all men were even as I myself. But every man hath his proper gift of God, one after this manner, and another after that. I say therefore to the unmarried and widows, It is good for them if they abide even as I. 1 Corinthians 7:7, 8, KJV

In the same chapter, verses 17 and 32-35 also say a great deal about Paul's obvious feelings in this matter. Paul sees both singleness and the married state as a gift. He feels that all people have a gift for either marriage or celibacy. The apostle does not believe that the only value of marriage is the control of sexual license. Paul does believe marriage allows a divinely approved expression of sexual desire that is a part of the gift of creation. These verses are clear and to the point. It amazes me how various people try to explain them away. I have heard some ministers preach a series of sermons from 1 Corinthians and when they dealt with the seventh chapter they would, for instance, deal with verses 1-11 in one message. They would just read verses 7 and 8 but never refer to them in their message, preferring rather to exegete verses 1 through 6 very carefully. Others have blatantly said that Paul was just mistaken in these verses. Those who question these verses mention that Paul thought the world was coming to an end and since it did not, we ought just to disregard them. This is a curious position, since I have heard these same ministers say, "I believe the Bible, the whole Bible, and nothing but the Bible." In Matthew 19:10-12, Jesus likewise mentions single adulthood as being viable. He does not give singleness preferential treatment as Paul does, but it must be remembered it was an option that he, like Paul, chose.

Of course those who are widowed and divorced are single as well as those who have never married. Ezekiel 24 speaks of the widower Ezekiel. First Corinthians 7, Matthew 5, and Mark 10 should be studied in relation to the issue of divorce. The grief experienced with the loss of a mate, whether due to divorce or death, is much the same.

Divorce is certainly one of the focal points of bitterness and rancor in our society today. We would like to think that as people become better educated and more affluent, the divorce dilemma would somehow diminish and finally disappear. This, however, is not happening. All indications are that the divorce rate is higher today in our country than it has ever been and that it is getting higher each year. Many social analysts are saying that the probability of a new marriage being interrupted by divorce before either partner dies is nearly fifty-fifty!

Divorce is certainly not the ultimate failure, and Christian people who have gone or are going through it need to know that every hurt has a right to be healed. People need to know, in the midst of a divorce as well as during those difficult days and weeks that follow, that they are still God's children. None of us has the right to say we are the favored child, but we all have the right to claim God as Father.

Some people in some churches have treated divorced people as if they had committed an unforgivable sin. The Scripture says that "nothing can separate us from the love of God" (Romans 8:39, KJV). First Corinthians talks about people who have a divisive spirit as being in the very center of sin. In my ministry I have seen divisive, contentious Christians casting the first stones at divorcees. If they only knew the harm their pharisaical attitudes were doing, they would surely mend their ways. None of us knows all about divorce, not even those who have been through it. I do know this, however: that real Christians, when dealing with divorce, are not judgmental or vindictive, but compassionate!

There are many other verses that I feel have an implied relevance to singleness. In 1 Corinthians 12, beginning with verse 12, we have a discussion related to the diversity of gifts in the body of Christ. The discussion is set in the context of those parts of the physical body that do not come in pairs. Though we have two arms and two legs and two eyes, we only have one liver and one heart and one brain. The Scripture says that if any part of the body fails to fulfill its function, it adversely affects the functioning of the whole body. The single adult can understand and relate to this very well, for without the heart or the brain or the liver the corporate body would die. Some single parts of the body have to be there; likewise with the body of Christ, the New Testament Church.

Luke 15:4 and following is the parable of our Lord about the lost sheep. There were ninety-nine that were safe in the fold, but there was one, not two, but one, that was lost. The Scripture goes on to say that there is great joy and rejoicing when the one is brought home. The "ones" of our world have multiplied in recent years. Now the "ones" number in the multiplied legions, and many of the "ones" are lost. Many of the "twos" that are in the fold are becoming "ones" and are being forced out of the fold. This needs to be stopped. We need to find and keep the "twos" and the "ones" so there will be great rejoicing not only here, but also in heaven. Sometimes as we read this parable we see it through the eyes of the sheep owner. We subconsciously rejoice with the owner because in the end he has not lost anything. Perhaps we need more of the vision of the sheep. The sheep needs to be in the fold, wants to be in the fold, but somehow is lost. Think what rejoicing there is when the sheep and the fold are once again united. Single adults want to be with the ninety-nine. They do not want to be out on the mountain wild and bare, but rather, close to the Shepherd's tender care and within the bounds of the love of the Church family.

Over the years I have heard many people say that you are not complete until you find your mate. I note that in recent years some have found innumerable mates and still are not complete.

Colossians 2:9, 10 says that we find our completeness in Jesus
Christ. No mention is made of any addendum. Who is
there among us that would say Jesus or Paul was not complete?

Finally, in Matthew 22:34 and following, Jesus sums up
the law and the prophets by putting the emphasis on loving God
and loving your neighbor. "Neighbor" in the Greek text
is singular. The Bible says that we should not only reach out to,
but also love, the one.

Some say that Genesis 1:28, "Be fruitful, and multiply, and
replenish the earth" (KJV), obliges all of us to marry.
I disagree. We must keep in mind to whom the Lord was speaking.
If they had not been fruitful and multiplied, we would
have had a tremendous problem. Also, we must remember that
all of the Lord's commands are not to be in each instance
universalized. I also feel that in some parts of the world this
injunction has been carried out.

In Genesis 2:18 we find, "It is not good for the man to be
alone" (NASB). One might ask who is alone today? Many
that are married are alone. I once counseled a couple who had
not spoken to each other in years although they lived in
the same three-room house. Some single people are alone; some
married people are alone. I do not want to deprecate the
value of marriage in any way, for I believe it to be a wonderful
state for those who choose it and are happy in it. Conversely,
I do not want someone who is married to verbally bludgeon me
into a position that they would choose for me.

There is a growing number of ministers to single adults all
across our country. Many of them are not adequately
equipped for the position they hold. Some are wonderfully
equipped by their experience as a single adult or by an unusual
sensitivity that was given to them as a gift from God. Woe
unto the legalist who tries to be a single adult minister. People,
particularly singles, do not fit into neat formulas or long
lists of rules without having a part of their being excluded. The
legalist wants to take people, particularly singles, and
shove them into a mold and just turn them out one after another
like so many cookies. Singles just do not fit into molds.

Every single is different from every other single and no one should
be made to feel like a failure spiritually if he or she does
not "turn out" just as the single minister wants him or her to.
Single adult ministers ought to be a part of the team that
helps people find and develop their God-given gift to whatever
they might be and whatever course they might take.

I feel that creating a sense of family is a definite responsibility
of every single adult group. If the leadership is not moving
in that direction, they are moving in the wrong direction.
"Family," the "body of Christ," the "Church"; these are
critically important words, and the implications of them are
significant to single adult ministry.

The Bible says a lot about singleness. Much of it is very
positive. God has given everyone gifts. Bless you as you use yours
in his service and in his family.

Dr. Nancy A. Hardesty
Candler School of Theology
Emory University
Atlanta, Georgia

2
RESPONSIBILITY FOR SINGLENESS

One of my favorite prayers from the Proposed Book of Common Prayer ends with the petition: "Grant us strength and courage to love and serve you with gladness and singleness of heart."

The words leap from the page and remind me that I am glad that I'm single, I enjoy being single, I rejoice in my singlehood as God's perfect will and gracious gift in my life.

Until a couple of years ago I could not have said that and I would have felt like punching anyone else who did. I would have thought, "Who are they trying to kid? They are lying to themselves!" I did not want to be single. I thought I was the victim of the lower birth rate for boy babies and the high casualty rates of the Vietnam War. I felt as if God was playing a very dirty trick on me. After all, I was a good Christian girl. I accepted Christ as my Lord and Savior, dedicated my life to God, prayed, read my Bible, went to church more than once a week and maintained my virginity. What more could God want? Did not my virtue deserve reward?

I was very lonely. Even the friends I had could not ease the pain I felt, nor could they really be there when I most needed someone. Sometimes the ache and the despair in the middle of the night led me to consider suicide. I didn't think life without a husband was worth living.

To some this sounds melodramatic and silly; but to others it sounds so similar to your own feelings that you will question my veracity when I say that after living with those feelings for about fifteen years I decided to change. Through friendship, spiritual growth, and therapy I have learned some things about loving and serving God "with gladness and singleness of heart."

A turning point came for me when I finally accepted responsibility for my singleness, when I realized that I had chosen and did choose to be single. I had fought that for a long time. Consciously I had always wanted to be married and saw myself as working toward that to the best of my ability. But one day a man I was dating declared, rather angrily, "You just won't do what it takes to get married." I knew he was right. I was not about to do what he had in mind and I realized that on a deeper level I had made many choices which lessened my chances of marriage.

I began to accept responsibility for and even enjoy the choices which I had made. I pursued a Ph.D. I was involved in and recognized as a leader of biblical feminism. I preferred to share most deeply in friendships with those who shared my Christian commitment rather than pursue someone simply because he was male and unmarried. There actually are many things in life which I do want more than marriage—and that is okay!

Singleness is not "second best"; being single is not equivalent to being a loser, even though many of us are brainwashed into that kind of thinking. "Old maid" was an epithet used to punish me from the time I was ten. On my fifteenth birthday I was given a booklet titled "How to Get a Husband for Christian Girls" which told me that "it is the abnormal girl who does not want marriage" and that all I had to do was "want it earnestly, every fiber of my being." I have heard even Christians assert that other Christians were single because "nobody would have her" or "he cannot get along with anybody." No wonder I felt singleness was a curse, a sign that I was an inadequate person, something bad for which I was to blame.

As I became aware of the choices involved in my singleness, I knew that I had sought God's guidance at every step. And God had heard me because God does love me and every other single person—those who are divorced, separated, widowed, as well as those who have never married. Our value as persons does not depend on others' evaluations of us, nor on their love or rejection. We too are worthwhile persons, made in God's image. Christ loved us enough to die for us and God continues to love us even when we sin. As Paul says, *nothing* can separate us from the love of God.

If you are separated or divorced, you undoubtedly made some choices, often very valid choices, which contributed to that. If you are widowed, you obviously did not choose to be; yet if you have been widowed for any length of time you have probably made choices about whether or not to seek remarriage. Each individual is responsible for these types of choices. Making those choices is part of the amazing freedom with which God endowed us at creation. If we *accept* responsibility for our choices, then if we are unhappy with the consequences of those choices, we can choose other options. We are not victims of life, puppets on God's or the Devil's strings. We have time and talents given us by God and we have the ability to change—painful and difficult as that may be. If singleness seems a prison, it is one we have chosen; we are bound by locks of our own devising. In Christ we have the power to be free.

For many singles the number one problem is loneliness. Rita Coolidge and Kris Kristofferson have a song titled "Help Me Make It Through the Night." Often the nights are the hardest: the streets are unsafe, the 24-hour supermarket is the only place open anyway, and it is too late to call even the best of friends. I used to cry and pray and read the Psalms—and still feel all alone. I have had people tell me that "Jesus is sufficient to meet all your needs" and I have sung that song about "falling asleep in the arms of Jesus" but that never was sufficient for me. This led to guilt trips about the depth of my spiritual life until I realized that God never intended to meet all our needs—that is why God created more than one person.

Loneliness can be changed—if one wants to conquer it. For a long time I wallowed in self-pity: "Poor me, I am all alone when everyone else has somebody." At times I enjoyed that self-pity but it did nothing to help my problem. I also took refuge in other people's evaluations of my situation: "You are single; you must be lonely. Does it bother you to eat alone?" Well, actually I am not and it does not. I finally realized that I did not need to apologize for or hide the fact that I really do enjoy my own company, enjoy having the house totally quiet when I read, enjoy scheduling my own time. I even enjoy cooking whatever I want for myself. And as my mother has learned since she has been widowed, having dinner across a TV tray from Walter Cronkite can be fun.

Being single does not mean being without relationships, even relationships of depth and duration. God created every human being for love—though not necessarily for marriage. We are created in the image of a triune God, three persons in deepest reciprocal intimacy. Most every person longs for intimacy whether that is defined sexually or nonsexually. Heterosexual marriage is *not* the only relationship nor even the most basic one. The companionship of friendship is more elemental. Friendships of all sorts and depths are available to single persons to meet a variety of needs.

The church was established as a Body, a family in which all are loved and accepted by God's grace whether Jew or Gentile, black or white, male or female, rich or poor. Ken Medema speaks of what the church was meant to be when he writes:

You're in my family,
In Christ you're kin to me
Now you are one with me,
*Shall we learn to be friends?**

*"Shall We Learn to Be Friends?" Fox Music Publications. Copyright 1977.

For many single people—people who outgrow the "College and Career Class" and do not become eligible for the "Young Marrieds," those who are divorced in midlife, those who are widowed after being active in the church as a "couple" for twenty years—the church is the most lonely place in their world. There is no appropriate Sunday school class, they sit alone in worship services, and go home alone, more lonely than when they came.

What can the church do? There seem to be two schools of thought: segregate and integrate. Some singles really want and need separate programs: single parent groups on a weeknight, a Sunday school class on grief-processing or improving interpersonal skills, a Sunday evening social and service group. At periods in my life I have participated in such groups, even started one, and think the church can minister to a very needy group of people *if that is what singles want*. Single people are adults; we do not need paternalistic married people programming "something good for us." At the moment, however, I participate in the life of two congregations where there is little distinction between singles and marrieds, where classes on a variety of interesting topics are open to everyone, where I can serve as I choose to and be served when I need to be. Both churches have a high proportion of single people of all categories who feel comfortable, lovingly accepted, needed, and cared for. At this stage in my life I prefer that to special treatment.

The church can help, but only the lonely person can actually cure his or her loneliness. It *is* a curable disease. I used to think relationships were a type of miracle, made in heaven. Friendships certainly are gifts from God, sent in answer to our prayers. They also must be worked at. Skills for achieving intimacy can be learned: I know because I did not have any, and over a period of years through therapy, reading, and trial-and-error I've learned a few (ask some of my friends and they'll be happy to tell you the lessons I have yet to learn!).

Intimacy requires risks. Everybody who risks makes mistakes sometimes. I certainly have made them. Taking risks means getting rejected sometimes. That does not mean you are a bad person or an inadequate person. We learn from our mistakes, pick ourselves up, dust ourselves off, and risk again.

Which leads me, by a certain logic, to the topic of sex. In case you haven't heard, sexual ethics and practices have been changing lately. Yet the church for the most part—a few denominational bodies, even fewer local congregations—has not begun to deal with issues of single *adults* sexuality. Most groups are still working with the question of "why wait until marriage?" when less than 50 percent of nineteen-year-olds are virgins and a sizeable number in the congregation are saying, "But I *was* married for ten, fifteen, or twenty-five years and now I'm single; what do I do about my sexuality?" I've heard well-meaning people voice the assumption that all singles are simply people with low sex drives. That may be true for some but it has never been true of me. I've had singles—from a twenty-six-year-old never-married to a middle-aged divorcee to a past-retirement-age widow—say to me through tears, "Maybe I am just oversexed."

God created sex and said it was good. One can now find shelves full of books lauding the joys of sexual expression (in marriage). God created each of us as sexual persons, as integrated persons of body, mind, and spirit. We are meant to be whole and happy people. That means that single adults have all the sexual needs and desires that married people have—and maybe more since we usually have no regular sex life. Our sexual feelings are not something we should be ashamed of or feel guilty for having or hesitate to talk to God and others about. Sexuality is a part of being alive. Repressing or denying those feelings only leads to anger, frustration, and fatigue.

Realizing the fact that I am a very sexual person has never been difficult for me—I have known that since I was ten —though in times of extreme pain I have prayed God to lobotomize that part of my brain. Coming to terms with my sexuality has been another matter. Again a crucial issue was that of choice. For a long time my moral behavior was dictated by traditional Christian morality. When I enviously watched the

behavior of some of my non-Christian friends, I felt that
my Christian commitment was more a punishment or a prison
than a joy. Eventually I faced up to the fact that I did not *have to*
comply with what other Christians (usually married) might
consider "proper" behavior. The choices were mine; the choices
I had made in the past had not been forced on me but had
been mine too. And I could either accept responsibility for those
choices and take pride in them or I could change my choices
in the future. Realizing that lifted a great burden of "ought" and
"should."

I also began to realize that my sex life or lack thereof was
not a measure of my worth or attractiveness as a person.
As I dealt positively with my own lack of self-esteem and began to
love myself more, my need for sexual affirmation lessened.
As I became more secure in myself, my lack of genital sexual
expression bothered me less. I was more able to sort out what were
really "sexual" needs from other legitimate needs for
caring, hugging, holding, stroking, affection, warmth. I found
that many of what I had formerly considered "sexual needs"
could be met in the non-sexual intimacy of friendship. That did
not solve the problem entirely, but it certainly made life
a lot easier.

And so I rejoice and give thanks that God's will for my life now
and perhaps always is not marriage. I know that God loves
me and that God loves you totally as we are: never-married,
separated, divorced, or widowed. We are, or can be, in the center
of God's will for our lives. If God has led you as God has
led me to choose the single life, then it is God's highest and best
will for us. Even if you feel as if you have gotten to where
you are by botching up your life, God specializes in making
beautiful mosaics from broken pieces. God's computer is
programmed for infinite variety. God can take us from where we
are this moment and lead us into happiness, maturity, and
fulfillment.

Our singleness, our time on earth, our talents, our sexuality,
are God's gifts to us, good gifts, loving gifts. Our choices,
our life-work, our relationships are our service to God, our gifts

back to God. God, "grant us strength and courage to love and serve you with gladness and singleness of heart." Are you willing to accept the responsibility for your singleness?

Margaret Dunbar
University of New Mexico Medical School
Albuquerque, New Mexico

3

LOVE, SEX, AND THE SINGLE

I have attended many conferences and seminars concerning "Sex Education and the Christian Single." Most of these speakers frustrated me because they never gave realistic answers. They wanted to talk about birds, bees, and weather. I desire to relate some *realistic* ideas concerning sex!

Sex and love! Are these terms synonymous? Indeed they are not, and yet they certainly can be. From a moral perspective, sexual intercourse is an expression of love, but love is so much more. The word "love" is so misused. The English language uses only one word "love" to mean the feeling of love for parents, friends, mate, or God. The Greek language has four words to verbalize the dimensions of love. The Greek words leave no doubt as to which type of love you are expressing.

The first love is *storge*, which is the love of family. It is basically a love of parent-child, but all of our "blood relatives" have an influence on *storge*-love. We came into the world not knowing how to love, thus our parents and family taught us to love. Many people are able to express love by touch and need the warmth of an embrace. Others have learned to love through the spoken word. Both are genuine expressions of love. If, by chance, you feel your parents failed or did not teach you to love, take time right now to forgive them. Then ask God to

forgive you for any bitterness you have for your parents
and kinsmen. *Storge* is the foundation upon which we build our
life of love.

As naturally as water flows in a river the next step in love is
that of *phileo*, the love of a friend. Since love is a commitment,
phileo-love develops at different levels. If you will seek
God's will concerning the depth of friendships, there will be fewer
heartaches. With God guiding, your friendships will be
established by true love. There will be many casual friends whom
we love but with whom we do not want anything beyond the
casual love-relationship. There will also be several close friends.
The *phileo*-love is deeper, more committed. When your
paths come together, you seek to spend time with one another.
However, there will be no desire for personal time to spend
with these friends. Lastly, we will have a few deeply committed
love relationships. In this there is a yearning for quality
time together, for talking over a cup of coffee, for sharing and
praying together.

A well-balanced life will have both men and women in every
area of commitment. God talks more about love between friends
than any other love. Ecclesiastes 4:9-12 shows what happens
when two or even three friends deeply love. The last part
of verse 12 declares, "three is even better, for a triple-braided
cord is not easily broken" (TLB). This is not a triangle but
a three-way love. When this three-way love is observed, it will
amaze others.

We have not been taught enough about this great love. Learn
the *importance* of a friend's love. Make a commitment to be a
friend, instead of expecting a romantic love. Perhaps one
day at the right time, a friendship love (*phileo*) may blossom into
a romantic *eros*-love.

Eros is the love of a mate. It is defined as tender, passionate
affection for one of the opposite sex. This love is one of the
greatest gifts and requires the deepest commitment. *Eros*-love
has some real dangers. It is easy to look at a mate as though
he or she is God. Just as easily, we may allow a mate to come
between us and God. An *eros*-love is a continuous, growing,

dynamic love which is never totally complete, yet becomes more meaningful. For those whom God has called into marriage, this love is ordained by and pleasing to God.

The greatest of all love is *agape*. You can love anyone with *agape*-love. This is divine love, loving as God loves. God loves us *as we are*. Thus we love all persons as they are, not asking them to conform to what we think they should be.

Knowing and understanding all four dimensions of love will aid in understanding sex. In dealing with sexual desire, a single adult has several options. Some of these options are Scriptural, while others are not.

1. Pretend the desire does not exist. This option is tried by many. It places an immense guilt trip on an individual. In the first place, by pretending the desire does not exist, you are saying you should not be experiencing any desire. That is not true. Sexual desire is God-given. It is a part of physical maturity. In the second place, such a pretense is lying, to yourself, if to no one else. Lying compounds this by making you feel guilty. It is really an option which is unreal and makes life miserable. Admit to yourself you do have sexual desire. Realize God gave you the desires, and talk to him about the sexual desires. He understands! He knows! He cares!

2. Take a cold shower to reduce the desire. This option, at best, is a very temporary relief. It offers no release from a desire which if not controlled can consume you. In addition there will be many times when there is no cold shower available. Besides, who wants a body that looks like dish-pan hands from many cold showers?

3. The third option is to find a consenting person and have sex. Remember sexual desire is God-given and good. Sexual desire is only a problem or evil when it possesses you. When you yield to your sexual desire, you have lowered what is good to a low, animal nature. You will also probably experience deep guilt. Please remember if you do yield to your passion the quickest way out of the valley of guilt is forgiveness. Ask God to forgive you, ask the one you injured to forgive you, and then forgive yourself. If you continue this option your conscience

will be dulled, you will begin to justify, you will begin to lie. One sin leads to another and soon you are deeply mired in the mud of sin. You may find this like quicksand which will pull you under and perhaps totally destroy your life.

Once again you will experience relief, not release. For in a very short time your burning sexual desire will return. You will be in a vicious cycle: sin, guilt, seeking forgiveness (for a time), uncontrolled desire, sin, guilt, etc. You will find self-satisfaction a very fast road to self-elimination.

A quick look into the Word will reveal this option is not for you. Colossians 3:1-5 (TLB): "Since you became alive... set your sights on the rich treasures and joys of heaven....*Let heaven fill your thoughts*....Away then with sinful earthly things; have nothing to do with sexual sin...." It is obvious from this that to be truly alive, we must abstain from sexual sin. This option leads to heartache, misery, and a life void of true happiness.

4. A fourth option is masturbation. I can find no place in Scripture that says, "Masturbation is a sin." There are widely differing opinions about this. I believe Satan wins many battles because we are unwilling to discuss this subject. In our society, it is a "no-no" even to mention masturbation. There are several ideas which will produce some positive thinking.

Masturbation is usually accompanied by fantasy of a sex act with another person. Matthew 5:28 (KJV) states, "But I say unto you, That whosoever looketh on a woman to lust after her hath committed adultery with her already in his heart." Can you then masturbate and not sin? Colossians 3:23 (KJV) says, "and *whatsoever* you do, do it heartily, as unto the Lord...." Can you masturbate, giving glory to the Lord? Can you praise God while you masturbate? Can you masturbate as unto the Lord? Christ is coming back to take us home with him. Would you want Christ to return and take you home while you are masturbating? That should be a sobering thought.

Statements are made that *all* men and 80 to 85 percent of women have masturbated. I do not like the word "all." There *are* people who have not masturbated, including some

men. If you have never masturbated, please do not be
critical of others. I believe it is time for us to understand some
of the underlying apparent needs. The physiological reason
most men masturbate is due to the pressure that is present as the
semen fluid builds. For many men the pressure is actually
painful. Masturbation releases this pressure—but, again, it is a
vicious cycle.

When men are being tested for possible infertility, they are
asked to abstain from any sex for a given period. In studies on
men undergoing these tests, it was discovered that if a
man abstains, the pressure will begin to be lessened due to
absorption of the fluid. Moreover, God has provided for
this psycho-physiological need by providing nocturnal emissions.
These are also known as "wet dreams." My brothers, if you
will allow God to care for you, at the time of need and
accompanied by a pleasant dream, the semen fluid will be
released, very naturally. There will be no sin or guilt involved.

Many if not most women who masturbate do so to keep from
yielding to sexual desire. Masturbation does not provide any
permanent help. It is at best a temporary relief and not
a release from sexual desire. The danger of masturbation is that
it can become a practice or habit which is hard to break.
A habit of masturbation before marriage can be carried into
marriage and destroy the marriage. You may say, if there is
sexual satisfaction in a marriage, masturbation will automatically
cease. Do not be deceived! This is *not* true in *all* cases.

With this knowledge of masturbation do you feel that
masturbation is an option? Or is it one of the ugliest deceptions
brought to us by Satan?

5. A fifth option is homosexuality. This option is identical
to that of option number three: sexual sin. Homosexuality is dealt
with in Scripture. Leviticus 18:22; 20:13, and Romans 1:26, 27
are three of the powerful Scripture references concerning
homosexuality. It is stated to be an abomination, but so is that of
heterosexual sin, sin of anger, and the sin of greed. In fact,
the abomination of homosexuality is spoken of only three
times, while the abomination of heterosexual sin is declared six

times. *All* sin is expressed to be an abomination many, many times.

There is so much published about homosexuality, and most of it seems to say hate-hate-hate the homosexual. It is time for us to look with *agape* love at those trapped in this perversion. Jesus came to set the captives free and *he can free them*. Jesus hated the sin but loved the sinner. Look at John 8:7-11, the story of the woman taken in adultery. Jesus showed us a self-righteous, judging crowd. This could just as well have been a woman caught in the act of homosexuality. Jesus told her, "Go, and sin no more." Jesus showed the love we can have. We will show far greater love by not condemning. With the gentleness of love, we can allow gays to know we love (*agape*) them.

Homosexuality can have devastating effects on the individual as well on the home. In many of the gays I have known I find a lack of commitment, much self-justification, and lying. This life-style is one of role playing even when the person has come out of the closet and declared himself to be gay. The gay seems to have a stereotyped perspective of what he or she believes society expects him or her to be.

As long as we hate homosexuals, they will not know that they can be healed. Homosexuality is not an unpardonable sin. It *is* forgiveable and the homosexual can be healed! It is not an easy road for them. They will find it difficult to pray for a healing from something they have enjoyed.

This option is taken by some out of pure rebellion. As the homosexual prays for forgiveness and to be set free he or she must realize there are other sins to be confessed. Ex-gays who are now happily straight state that three additional sins which they had to confess were rebellion, pride, and self-pity.

Homosexuals need a friend, one to whom they can pour out their deepest thoughts and feelings of their hearts. They need to know that this friend will love, love, love, and not condemn or judge.

An option is the exercise of a power of choice. Thus

homosexuality would have to be classified as an option. However, an option of homosexuality is life-destroying. To be free from this option the person will need lots of love, to be immersed in the Word, and to be surrounded with loving, non-judgmental Christian friends. There may be failure, just as there is in dealing with anything which controls you. Homosexuality is often a compulsion stronger than alcoholism, drug addiction, overeating, or gambling. The homosexual must be challenged to be an optimist, not a pessimist. A pessimist sees a problem in every situation. An optimist sees an opportunity in every problem. Use the failures as opportunities to grow closer to God, as you seek him.

6. The sixth option is to commit the sex desire to God! For me, the sixth alternative is the only way for true happiness. This is an option that is well pleasing to God. It builds a lifetime of love, security, peace, joy, and happiness. What a difference!

I have been single for several years. I now enjoy every minute of the gift of singleness. As 1 Corinthians 7:7 says, "I wish everyone could get along without marrying, just as I do. But we are not all the same. God gives some the gift of a husband or wife and others, he gives the gift of being able to stay happily unmarried" (TLB). Jesus says in Matthew 19:11 that all men cannot accept the lot of singleness, only those to whom it is given. If Jesus says it is given, then I have a very special gift from my Savior.

How did I become a happy single? It was not easy, but God taught me every step of the way. First of all, according to Psalms 139:13-16, God made me exactly as he wanted me! He formed my unique personality and character. He even allowed a beautiful Christian woman to carry me in her womb until God's handwork was complete.

The next step toward happiness was my family's influence as I grew up on a farm and ranch in Colorado. I had two older sisters and an older brother, all of whom delighted in teasing me. I learned to tease in return. We had many fun-filled hours and knew real love. It was our evenings which taught us to love and understand each other since these were times of study or

family fun. During these years, I learned a lot of self-discipline.
Cows had to be milked at specific times, and ranch chores
required early hours. My father used to laugh and tell everyone
that we were born in a saddle and I believed him when I
spent twelve to fifteen hours some days on a horse herding cattle.

My mother was a beautiful Christian and I appreciate the
influence she had on my life. My maternal grandmother was a
very assertive Christian and the times she lived with us gave her
an opportunity to share Christ with me. My father was not a
Christian until shortly before his death. There was a country
Sunday school, but because of my father's rebellion we often were
not allowed to attend. This had an impact on my life and
probably partially influenced my not becoming a Christian until I
was twenty.

I recognize that many times I was controlling my own life. For
instance, when I began to date and agreed to marry my former
husband, I did not seek counsel from God nor my parents. I
simply announced I was going to get married. In open rebellion,
I married him when I was eighteen. While we were married
three children were born—a son and two daughters, each of
whom has trusted Christ as his or her Savior.

When it was evident that our marriage was finished, I knelt
beside my bed and asked God what he wanted me to do.
I was impressed that I was to become a Medical Technologist.
Wanting to be sure, I asked God to confirm this to me.
The Lord was faithful in answering and confirming his will. A
peace flooded my soul and there were never any doubts.
I realized that I needed to change locations so that I could attend
college. Some people tried to discourage me from this
drastic step of attending college because they felt it was
impossible with three young children. When this discouragement
arose, I remembered God's confirmation and, with his help,
I could see the victory. God helped me get the necessary degree
in record time. I am now teaching Medical Technology
at the University of New Mexico Medical School in Albuquerque.

Pastors, friends, and loved ones have influenced my life
and encouraged me in the happiness I have found. But, most of

all, Jesus has been teaching me each day. When some people see me so radiant they are sure there must be a man in my life, and there is: Jesus Christ. Often people tell me that I am the happiest person they know. Now, there is a sparkle, laughter, joy, peace, and an assurance of God's love. I could ask for no greater happiness.

All areas of my singleness have not been without struggle. Yet, with each struggle comes victory! One of the major battles in my life has been the struggle and victory in the area of sexual desire. In no other area of life has God given more specific directions than in the area of adultery and fornication.

Adultery is sexual sin between a married man and another man's wife. Fornication is sexual sin of a single man and woman. The Scripture which has been the most powerful in my life is that of Ephesians 5:1-4 (TLB): "Follow God's example in everything you do. . . .Be full of love for others, following the example of Christ. . . .Let there be no sex sin, impurity or greed among you. Let no one be able to accuse you of such things." We are to follow Christ's example. And, Christ was tempted in all ways, as we are, yet without sin (Hebrews 4:15). His example is to draw strength from temptation and be stronger for having been tempted. Certainly God is true to his promise of 1 Corinthians 10:13 (NASB), "No temptation has overtaken you but such as is common to man; and God is faithful, who will not allow you to be tempted beyond what you are able; but with the temptation will provide a way of escape also, that you may be able to endure it."

God is faithful! He never goes back on a promise. Just as God has been faithful in my life, he will do the same for you. Research has revealed that the peak of sexual desire and of activity usually is between the ages of twenty-five and thirty-five. I was twenty-eight when I started to college, right in the middle of the peak of my sexual desires. The first two years were busy, happy years with only minimal problems. However, in my third year of college, my senior year, I began to experience a tremendous sexual desire. My first response was to take it to God. I asked him to take this desire from me. It did not

happen!! The desire intensified. I knelt beside my bed each
night and begged, pleaded, implored. I even demanded God to
take the desire from me. He did not. But he did provide
a way of escape. Getting a degree in three years with my three
very small children meant I got only four to six hours of
sleep each night. I wrestled with this desire nightly but was so
tired that I soon fell asleep. The desire was increasing
and literally possessing me. I would not submit and fall into sin.
Praise God! He did help me.

The desire was so strong that I was considering seeking a
doctor to see if there was any medication which would
permanently destroy the sexual desire. It was radical but I
desperately needed help. While I was considering this,
God sent the help I had been needing.

God's help came in the form of a televised Billy Graham
crusade. I have no idea what his text was, but I shall never forget
that night. In the middle of his sermon, Dr. Graham suddenly
said he wanted to step aside from his message and talk to the
teenagers in the audience. Being old enough to be a teenager
twice over, I listened intently. He told us that sexual desire is
given to us by God. God gives only good gifts; therefore,
these feelings are good, normal, and healthy. But you can give
the desires to God for safekeeping until you marry.

What an impact! I gently bowed my head and told God I wanted
to give my sexual desires to him. A peace flooded me and
I knew I no longer would be possessed by my sexual desires. The
peace that flooded my soul was a spiritual knowledge
which was similar to that which I experienced when I trusted
Christ as my Savior. I rejoiced in this knowledge. I completed
the telecast, although I remember nothing else from the
sermon. For the first time in my college career I went to bed
before my studies were completed. I went instantly to sleep
and had the most blessed night of sleep I have ever experienced.

The next day, Sunday, my family was playing "exchange
the grandchildren." I had to drive about a hundred miles to meet
my oldest sister. At that time in my life, I was a very legalistic

Christian. I could not, for fear of God's wrath, miss Sunday
school or Morning Worship. At that time, I felt that I could not
worship anywhere except in a church of my own denomination.
I thought we were not going to find one, but at last we located a
small church of the "correct" denomination. The Sunday
school teacher mentioned having heard the same Billy Graham
telecast. She related what he had told the teenagers. I
silently thanked God for taking my desires, and I thanked God
that it was for everyone, not just teenagers.

I did not understand what had happened that night and the next
day, but I continued to rejoice that I had been set free.
Several years later, I was asked to serve on a panel for a singles
group. My topic was "Sex and the Single." I went to God
for direction and knew I was to share my testimony, even though
I did not fully understand all that happened.

One morning the Lord awakened me at two o'clock as he
frequently does. This particular morning the answer came. It is so
simple:

*I was really guilt-ridden because I had sexual desires. I had
never stopped to realize that these desires were normal. Had God
taken my desire before the guilt was removed, it would have
been devastating. I would probably have had an emotional breakdown and no one would have understood why. It is like an
ugly, deep cut that is sutured without cleaning and heals at the
top. It will explode until healing and cleansing begins in
the depth of the wound.*

*I was suddenly free from guilt when I gave my desires to Jesus.
I did not ask, plead, or demand him to take them. God does
not forcibly "take" anything from anyone. He takes our lives, our
desires only when we give them to him.*

*Sunday morning was an extremely important time. When I
prayed Saturday night, I did not thank God for his work. When I
thanked God on Sunday, my commitment was sealed.*

Spiritual victories sometimes have no immediate measure-
ment, except that of inner peace. As time continues, we will

observe the proof. My victory was tested and proven over and over.

God was faithful. He kept all his promises to me. First Thessalonians 4:3, 4 (KJV) says: "For this is the will of God, even your sanctification, that ye should abstain from fornication: that every one of you should know how to possess his vessel in sanctification and honour." It was God's will for me to be free from the land of bondage. He set me free to live in liberty. He will do the same for you.

I am free of the tormenting desires. It happened to me instantly. Perhaps for others it might be slower, and happen over a period of time. I am very much a woman, and enjoy every day as a single woman. It is an exciting life for now I can date, have close male friends, visit with men, and know the peace God has given me.

Since I first shared my testimony, I cannot count the men and women who have come to me with thanksgiving. They know I have done nothing but speak for God. They too, have found sexual freedom: freedom and deliverance from sexual sin and desires.

If God has our sexual desires and drives, we can be tempted, but without any effect. Try God and his promises and enjoy life to its fullest excitement.

Dr. Jim Towns
Department of Communication
Stephen F. Austin State University
Nacogdoches, Texas

4

ONE IS NOT
A LONELY NUMBER

Finding out who you are is perhaps the most agonizing yet beautiful task of your life. It is a lifetime journey. I am a person who has never married, yet I'm not a second-class citizen. I have learned to be alone but not lonely! As a flesh-and-blood human being, I feel, I think, I am happy, and I hurt. I am a vital person. I resent the societal connotations of being "single." I am very much a part of life and life is very much a part of me.

The only difference between a married person and a single is that marrieds are living life with a spouse; singles are meeting life head-on, alone. We all do the same things, such as breathe, eat, sleep, work, play, and talk. Properly adjusted singles are not anyone's "better half," they are their own well-balanced whole. Do not misunderstand; I am not antimarriage!

I don't know if I will remain single all my life. But for me, marriage must not be an "escape" from singleness. If I were to marry, I know that I would be as happy as I choose to be —regardless of conditions. I am learning the deep meaning and peace of being able to say with Scripture, "I have learned, in whatsoever state I am, therewith to be content" (Philippians 4:11, KJV). Happiness is not dependent on circumstances but upon attitudes. Perhaps God has some special opportunities for me that would enable me to relate and assist others, opportunities that would not be possible if I were married.

For a long time singles have been viewed as marginal members of a couple-oriented society. Suddenly, singleness is okay and single people count. They are a new social class. Single adults are persons! Rather than being a member of one group called "single," they are members of multiple categories. Singles may be classified as never-married, separated or divorced, widow or widower. Regardless of the label, a single is a person of value, dignity, and worth. It is a mistake to classify all single adults together. Each one has his own life-style, background, and personality. There is no "typical" single person. Life-styles and perspectives are as different as individuals or fingerprints.

There are three inaccurate assumptions concerning non-marrieds: 1) there is something wrong with them either socially or sexually; 2) they have a carefree "swinger" or "anything goes" life-style; and 3) they are unsettled and irresponsible.

A single can also be efficient and productive because of the goals set to channel his or her capacities and energies. Many singles accomplish goals which could not be achieved if they were restrained by immediate family ties. Both marrieds and singles appear to be suffering from a kind of "grass is greener on the other side of the fence" syndrome. Whatever their marital status, many people look at others as if they "had it made." If the grass is greener on the other side of the fence, you can be sure of these things—the water bill is higher and tall grass is hard to mow. In my association with people, it appears that for every single who wishes he or she were married so all his or her problems would be solved, there is a married person who thinks that being single again would solve all problems.

Married people are usually described as more "mature" or "adult," although many single people are far more mature and resourceful than some married people. Marrieds are usually thought of in terms of what he or she has, while singles are often described in terms of what he or she does not have. The

label "single" is difficult for most people to define except in
negative terms such as "spouseless" or "not married."
Dinner parties and most social occasions are comprised of six or
eight people. The odd-numbered guest often feels like a
third thumb. Many social events are geared to "couples" and
"family night suppers." These are the rule rather than the
exception. Yet, one is *not* a lonely number!

The "all-American single" is supposed to be happy,
competent, and successful. Yet, with most singles there is a war
going on between aloneness versus loneliness. Everywhere
I go conducting conferences and speaking, I find people of all
ages and backgrounds wanting to find help in adjusting to
aloneness and dealing with loneliness.

There is a vast difference between "loneliness" and
"aloneness." All of us need times when we can be alone to
reassess values, priorities, and a sense of direction. Loneliness
happens because a person lacks the inner resources to be
alone. In other words, loneliness is a longing for companionship
or a feeling of isolation by being away from others in a
despairing way.

Robert Weiss, in his book *Loneliness*, has revealed a
distinction between two kinds of loneliness. There is "emotional
isolation" which results from the loss or lack of a truly
intimate tie (usually with spouse, lover, parent, or child). There
is also a "social isolation" which is the consequence of
lacking a network of involvements with peers of some kind such
as family and friends. It appears that emotional loneliness
is coming to grips inside oneself about being alone. Social
loneliness is desiring companionship.

Most people have experienced both kinds of loneliness at
one time or another. Loneliness is not exclusive to the single life.
At the conclusion of Robert Weiss' book, he states: "I can
offer no method of ending loneliness other than the formation of
new relationships that might repair the deficit responsible
for the loneliness. And I think this solution ordinarily is not easy.
If it were, there would be fewer lonely people." Perhaps
the most profound statement concerning loneliness is that no one

ever takes the place of anyone else, yet there are new places created. We must *use* aloneness and *deal with* loneliness. We *need* aloneness; God wants us to *triumph* over loneliness.

There is a dynamic, positive aspect of loneliness—it can cause me to want a continuing right relationship with God and other people. When I am alone I have the opportunity to do some very important things: 1) Reflect. I can rethink that which has happened and meditate. 2) Evaluate. This gives me an opportunity to sort things out and determine what is really going on. 3) Grow. While alone I have a chance to go through the decision-making process concerning the alternatives. This provides a healthy format for personal growth. While I am alone doing these things, I have a deeper comprehension of what Scripture means in saying, "Be still, and know that I am God" (Psalms 46:10, KJV). Some people never know because they are never still!

To many single adults loneliness means failure and rejection. It means that you did not make it; you are no good. In counseling with people, I have decided that the deepest pain in loneliness is caused by an awareness of "I'm not wanted" or "I'm not loved." The proper mind-set of the well-adjusted single is to be alone without being lonely. We need to turn loneliness into being alone and appreciate the value of being alone. A person's self-concept and self-acceptance plays an important role in *handling* loneliness and *using* aloneness.

The words of Paul Tillich come to my mind while I am talking with lonely people. "It is easy to be lonely but it is difficult to be alone." It has already been stated that loneliness is not the same as being alone. Aloneness is the creative way of being alone and liking it! Loneliness is an unwelcomed separation from other people.

Some people enjoy being alone, while others dread it. Since "alone" means the physical thing of being all by yourself, "loneliness" is psychological regardless of how many people are around you. The ability to be creatively, happily alone is a very healthy status to obtain.

A number of strange, incorrect ideas have emerged in our

society. The first is that Christians with enough faith are never lonely. However, a Christian is subject to all human attributes and feelings. The second idea is that single people are the most lonely. In counseling, I have found that many married people are as lonely as the single people I know. Singleness can be lonely at times, yet what about the spouse who is alienated from his mate and only negative words are exchanged? That's loneliness!

As an individual becomes more mature, the more creative he or she can become in the use of this time alone. An understanding of healthy aloneness is self-love, yet not in a selfish sense. It is best exemplified in the person who likes himself and is comfortable with himself. Aloneness is an art form, a discipline, and a science.

There are several helpful hints for turning loneliness into aloneness:

1) Accept the fact that at times you are going to be lonely. Recognize your feelings and deal with them. Are you willing to be alone—even single? As you accept the fact that you will be lonely at times, you can look forward to something as you plan ahead, and yet enjoy today.

2) Realize that feeling lonely is not abnormal. It is very normal that all people will be lonely during certain times. Being lonely is not right or wrong. The feelings of loneliness can be okay. This is a time when you can increase your estimate of your value, worth, and dignity. During this time do something that you have really been wanting to do. Perhaps you would enjoy something physical such as athletics, sports, or just walking.

3) Learn to be still at times. As you practice being still, your quiet-mindedness will help you to put your feelings in proper perspective. In other words, change your inner pace. It is possible to go fast outside yet be very calm inside.

4) Sharing your loneliness helps you to enjoy your aloneness. When you are lonely, this gives you an opportunity to relate to other lonely people. As you share your loneliness, you will find that you are not as lonely as you felt that you were.

It is a comfort to all people involved when loneliness is shared. When you feel lonely, go talk with someone who cares for you! When you are objective and honest in exchanging thoughts and feelings, you will find a healthy relationship with another person. As you do things for other people, you will find that you also receive! A practical suggestion for overcoming emotional alienation is to seek relationships with people with whom there can be mutual encouragement spiritually, and stimulation intellectually and socially. Therefore, there is a time for loneliness and there is a time for aloneness.

Dr. Sarah Frances Anders
Department of Sociology
Louisiana College
Pineville, Louisiana

5

SINGLE, SANE, AND SECURE

Singleness for me, as for many, has not been a state of mind so much as a state of being. It is not so much a matter of preoccupation as one of assumption. I was born single and have remained unmarried through the periods of choice, circumstance, and circulation! Unlike some maritally "unattached," I have seldom been self-conscious about that status either because of self or social pressures. I can recall feelings of smugness, as a high school senior, when my friend who was valedictorian announced that she would be marrying shortly after graduation. There was self-satisfaction and contentment that marriage for me would fall into a time sequence after educational plans were completed.

One commencement fifteen years later, when I was wearing a faculty robe rather than a senior one, I whispered to a colleague in the midst of an address that I hoped we would be out on time since I had to speak at a singles conference about twenty miles away. His surprised query: "Why are *you* going?" was genuine. Hesitation. Then, "Heavens, I never think of you as single." Even now I am not certain if that was a back-door affirmation of my normalcy or a friendly compliment! Admittedly, by this time two of my graduate degrees included an emphasis on the family. I had some sort of reputation for

being pro-family in teaching, research, and writing—I was even among those who were talking about the "single family."
My colleagues' acceptance of me as a person rather than a "single" was tantamount at that time to their considering me as one of the "fellows" on an almost all-male faculty!

All of which enforces my conviction that perhaps others (married or single) see you somewhat according to your own self-image. And I view myself as a single family, with most of the concomitant responsibilities, liabilities, *and* rewards that "family" usually implies. Granted, in a society that often rewards the nomadic soul who wants to move occupationally and geographically at frequent intervals, I have been an atypical single who tends to put down roots and regard each new professional site as "home."

SINGLE AND PROFESSIONAL

It has been my good fortune to have had two different professional experiences, neither of which stigmatized me as a single or a woman. By my mid-twenties, I was well into my third graduate degree in preparation for college teaching in the field of sociology, after having been on the staff of three southern churches in positions of music and education. Yet there were concerned friends and relatives who would ask the two perennial questions, usually seriously but occasionally in humor: "Are you *still* going to school?" (as if I were something of a slow learner!) and "Whatever happened to that last nice young fellow who was interested in you?" (as if I were collecting scalps or broken hearts!). While these questions were generally not intended to put me on the defensive nor to be rude, I admit I secretly made a collection of perfect comebacks, most of which I was either too polite or inhibited to use. I even considered, "Why ever did you get married?" and "Don't you ever feel the need for a little more education?"

My theological and sociological training also have contributed equally to my perspective for more than twenty years of leading college students in Bible study. Most of them have been

never-marrieds, knee-deep in determining not only the
direction of their vocational preparation but the nature of their
value systems. Nothing could be more exciting than to
watch young adults, eighteen to twenty-four years of age, learn
the importance of feeling fulfilled and secure as they examine
their religious beliefs, their vocational choices, and their
dating values. I cannot begin to enumerate the host who have sat
with me in Bible study, learning to grow in spiritual awareness,
weaning themselves from parental support, and refusing to
push the panic button on marriage before they have learned to be
secure in singleness.

There have been very few semesters in over two decades of
teaching sociology that I have not taught the ever-popular elective
course in Marriage and the Family. While this has been
a part of the degree requirements for our students in sociology
and social work, more than one-half of the students in nearly
every course have chosen it as one of only four or five elective
courses they have during their college careers. When I
first began to teach, almost all of the students were single and
hopeful. Yet none of the textbooks dealt with their singleness
except in the context of finding and taking a mate; very
few dealt with the plight, problems, or possibilities of the once-
marrieds. The assumption seemed to be that there was only
one normal life-style, and that any period of singleness was
abnormal and merely a transition into the marital state.
As the years passed, classes were about evenly divided between
the single, engaged, and recently married. Now the widowed,
divorced, and separated are increasingly visible participants.
Although more and more textbooks include chapters on
widowhood, divorce, and even restructured marriages, there are
scarcely more than three or four that consider the option
of remaining unmarried or using singleness as a viable family
life-style.

Surprising to many is the fact that the vast majority of my
students in Marriage and the Family seldom give thought to my
marital status or consider that it has any real bearing on
the content of the course. I still chuckle over the student several

years ago who volunteered that he had never expected his
religion professor nor his preacher to have committed all the
immoralities discussed in the Bible nor his doctor to have
all the diseases he diagnosed and kept up-to-date on—why
should he expect me to have been married, widowed,
separated, divorced, and remarried?

SINGLES AND PASSAGES

Long before Sears' *The Seven Ages of Man* or Sheehy's *Passages*,
I was teaching about the stages of life that are universal
to humankind and those that are uniquely ours. They are
certainly not laid out neatly in seven-year blocks of living—nor
even decades, as marked by becoming twenty-one, thirty,
forty or sixty-five. It seems in retrospect that my passages
coincided with four years of high school, a B.A. after
two-and-a-half more years, a year in a job, two more in seminary,
and so on. Achievements, geographical moves, and new
friends marked every phase.

What is significant is that the first three universal passages
are all part of singleness in our society: out of childhood,
into pre-puberty, and through adolescence. So often it appears
that socialization during these times does not so much help
one to be comfortable and happy in singleness, but rather to be
programmed for a certain kind of marriage. Being a year
younger than most of my classmates, I lagged a bit in the dating
game, so when I went off to college at sixteen I began to
pick up momentum. I made up for lost time! A little over two years
later with a diploma in hand and a lapsed engagement, I
still might have been voted one of "the most likely to be married
soon!" It never seemed that I was deliberately postponing
marriage as I moved from job to graduate school to job to graduate
school intermittently, for there were many rewarding and
promising relationships over that decade. But I sometimes say
(only half-facetiously) to an occasional young man or
woman who has been overly programmed for the happy-marriage

syndrome, "Do not despair, I had some of the most gratifying opportunities for marriage *after* thirty!"

We need to remind ourselves often that we not only are *born* single; the chances are strong that we may also have other periods of non-marriage. We may even make the final passage "singly." It may well be that the ultimate test of maturity is not how well we play the marriage game, but rather how well we cope with and use creatively the periods of singleness.

In retrospect, one might say that the twenties for me were single because there were other priorities, primarily educational. The thirties included some wonderfully warm and exciting relationships, but singleness was still a matter of deliberation, not an accident nor by default. There are now many additional responsibilities that have come with median adulthood, but I have found that major decision-making does not end with the first two decades of adulthood! Some of these perennial choices have concerned my profession—mostly to choose between administrative posts or remaining in the classroom. Except for one stint as interim dean, I have thus far opted for the faculty-student arena. I find enough administrative outlets in chairing a department, serving on significant committees on campus and abroad in the community and nation. About 20 percent of my time is concerned with writing, counseling, and speaking.

I have found a real extension of my classroom to be in community and denominational service. Most of the civic boards I participate in concern the family: family counseling, child protection, child guidance for the emotionally disturbed, and rehabilitation for the pre- and post-delinquent youth of our area. My church and denominational life is vital to me, not just through my Bible class on Sundays, but through conferences directed toward singles, family life, and Christian education. I do considerable writing on consignment in various religious and theological periodicals, as well as in sociological journals. I have written and contributed to books in religion and sociology. All of these interests make for a heavy schedule, but

I find them to be energizing rather than draining both spiritually and professionally. I am "in the air" once or twice per month and being an inveterate "people watcher," I find the en route encounters almost as rewarding as the conferences.

There are many responsibilities I value, such as my relationship with my two godchildren and the attention I give to my octogenarian blind mother. There are many former students over the years who have afforded me warm relationships with their children. I even have a namesake, Anders Christian, born to a young Danish couple I came to know well one summer when I stayed in Scandinavia. But the longest and most committed has been the relationship with my godchildren whose guardian is a remarkable single woman. Baptists are not traditionally given to godparent commitments, but I would wholeheartedly recommend such a spiritual and extended-family experience for other never-marrieds or for once-marrieds without children. Even if geographical distance permits only a few get-togethers a year, the ongoing ties bring many kinds of satisfaction.

Singles, particularly single women, often have the opportunity to care for their senior adult parents. This has been a unique passage for one who is the only living family member of a senior citizen as I am and who left home at sixteen, to return only for short visits over long stretches of time. Make no mistake, my life-style changed considerably after the second widowhood and declining health of my mother, who is a retired teacher. We sold the family property about five years ago and moved her into a duplex I own, where she had been energetic and independent until she recently lost her vision. Her determination to stay alert and reasonably independent after a lifetime of reading and community-church activity is a noteworthy example for all of us. We have become reacquainted over this period of geographical proximity and feel that we both should strive to maintain the best of our former life-styles. I shall continue some of my varied extracurricular activities and travels so long as good help and her health permit. We are excited about her "reading" the Bible and the classics again and again via talking books. We consider a convalescent home the last possible resource in our situation. Both of us are inclined to take each day as it comes, living it to the fullest within our mutual limitations.

SINGLES AND STEREOTYPES

As I participate in seminars and conferences for the never- and once-marrieds, I find them understandably resisting the numerous stereotypes that the married community often holds about them. I find few who resemble the swingle who is a composite of the life-style of Joe Namath, the looks of Julie Christie, and the spending patterns of Jackie Onassis! Nor are there many Born Losers among them, ultra-sensitive to their marital status and subject to spells of suicide-prone depression. In fact, over the past decade there has been a marked trend away from problems-oriented seminars for bright, gifted singles and a trend toward positive, creative discussions about rearranging life-styles for more productive and spiritual living.

More and more non-marrieds among the thousands I have encountered and questioned have appeared amused rather than bemused about the labels that are thrust upon them: frustrated, subnormal singles; destructive, desperate divorcée; devastated, crumpled widower. They see themselves as far more heterogeneous than married people, and *that is variety*! Many of them agree with my philosophy that one's energy is misspent in trying to refute such over-simplified descriptions or being irritated by them. No one, and especially the non-married, ought to go through life being a reactor; the challenges of most of our lives demand that we be actors, initiators, copers, assertors.

One of the grossest wrong assumptions about singles is that they lack family orientation. This idea discounts the two decades singles spend in their parents' family or the experiences, happy or otherwise, that they have for some time in their own. As a single I find that I often can relate to children better than

their mothers (partly because I do not have to be around
them all the time). My hospital experience during my pastoral
psychology training included a period in obstetrics and
pediatrics, which often prompts me to observe that I may well
have diapered and fed a greater variety of babes than
most married people! Once again, most singles do not regard
themselves as unattached to families, just uncoupled. One
frustration they voice is that the church and other groups fail to
recognize them as "families." Socially, they prefer not to
be isolated into separate subgroups for all of their contacts and
relationships. In the church, as a case in point, they want
to be a part of the church family, not just involved in the singles
ministry they may enjoy through Bible study and social activities.

BANES AND BLESSINGS

There is consensus among singles that the three greatest
problem areas are social, financial, and sexual. I would agree.
Years ago, singles felt even more stigmatized than I sense
is true today. But they still indicate at times that they feel like
fifth wheels or the odd half of a broken pair. There are
still single women who feel strange about going certain places
alone. Both men and women are good-humored about the
attempts of their friends at matchmaking; but men more than
women find that hostesses like their spare-chair status.

The non-married person can easily fall into unrewarding
friendships and alliances due to a scarcity of genuine peers or
out of loneliness, but that is not unique to singles. I feel
that the most limited view of friendship is that one's closest
associates must come from one's own social and marital
niche. I repeatedly stress that one of the greatest opportunities
a single has is in the wide variety of associations he or she
can maintain. Indeed, society is much more apt to criticize us if
we have too absorbing and exclusive friendships with one
person of either the same sex or the opposite sex. As I reflected
in my book, *Woman Alone: Confident and Creative*, my most
satisfying friendships over the past ten years have included an

octogenarian, a retired Shakespeare professor, a married
sociology alumna's family, the dean of an architectural school,
the foster mother of my godchildren, a single woman accountant,
a faculty colleague and his wife, and a comfortably-retired
couple in our church.

Since I am by nature and nurture a workaholic, my greatest
pitfall has always been overinvolvement in work I very
much love. Both professions I have been in would surely have
been miserable if I had not been "called," so it has been
very gratifying to me to feel this strong sense of *vocation*. I would
probably have difficulty with this tendency to work overtime
even if I were married, but I admit I am more vulnerable
as a single.

Except for tax-discrimination, the never-marrieds fare better
than average financially since they are generally better
educated and more mobile professionally. However, the next tax
revolt, after the vote on Proposition 13 in California,
may well be from singles! Divorced persons usually suffer more
financially because of separating common property between
two households. The divorcee may find herself going back to or
continuing in the job market at non-competitive wages—and
with children to support. Some expenses run disproportionately
higher for the unmarried; per capita food, shelter, transportation,
utilities, and insurance, for instance. I have been penalized
salary-wise in only one school and that was due as much
to my being a woman as to my marital status.

I am a healthy female with a normal heterosexual drive. I have
always regarded sex as one of many wholesome, necessary
biological needs. Failing to continually satisfy this urge certainly
has not been as devastating as ignoring the thirst or exercise
and rest drives would be. There has been no conscious effort to
sublimate sexual needs through other types of activities,
but my varied interests (music, golf, civic involvement,
speaking, et. al.) could be viewed by some neo-Freudians as
forms of unconscious sublimation! What do they say about
marrieds with the same interests? Most of the singles I encounter
are very open about their sexuality, but do not see it confined

to sex relations. Neither are they inclined to expect the church to permit them greater sexual freedom or provide a different morality for singles.

Singles collectively are doing a great many exciting things for our society. I suspect they contribute more financially, in service, and in brain power than we often realize. Furthermore, they offer happiness and fulfilment to others, even though some singles are not happy or fulfilled themselves. Like Bishop Fulton Sheen, I like to think of how many people I may have made happy by not marrying them—and perhaps how many I may have an opportunity to bless because I happen to be single!

Dr. Steve O'Kelly
Pastor to Single Adults
First Baptist Church
Houston, Texas

6

TOO MANY FRUSTRATED SINGLES

After pastoring single adults for over three years, I am convinced that it is not God's will that there be so many single adults in our generation. Statistics reveal that there are more single adults in this generation than ever before. I have been wondering why. Most of you could answer that question for yourself.

Before you form an inaccurate conclusion, I encourage you to read these ideas with openness. Some frustrated single adults have copped-out by trying to make themselves believe that they are meant to be single, when deep in their hearts they know that they do not have the gift of singleness. If you know that you have the gift of singleness, then these ideas are probably not directed toward you. Perhaps it is right and best for you to be single. Yet, consider the singles who actually have the gift of marriage.

If there is one prayer God could bless me with more than anything else, it would be that I would see many weddings among our singles. I am not saying that I think God has called us to be matchmakers. But, I am saying that I believe there is a singles' sickness in our generation. I believe that it could be so subtle that you might not realize you are a victim.

There is an appalling misinterpretation by some concerning being a single adult. Many times, due to inward struggles or problems, we have gone to the church, hiding behind a false interpretation that says, "If you are single, you can do more for the kingdom of God." I am not saying that a single person cannot do more for the kingdom of God. I believe a single person *can do* much if he or she is not frustrated. So, those of you who are not frustrated, do more for the kingdom of God! The rest of you, seek a mate and marry! Still, the greatest precaution is: Do not marry until you have found God's person for you.

There are certain cultural hindrances that have put some negative societal programming into the singles of our generation of which we must be on guard. We must ask for God's leadership and discerning power. Some programming appears in the form of negative priorities. Surely, the most positive scriptural priority is love for God, self, and others.

Too many of us feel a "funeral" in our hearts rather than life and love. God wants everyone to have inner peace. With all of life's futilities, I am convinced that there are some things that can bring life and love to pass. The most special ingredients of life is personal acceptance of Jesus and then self-acceptance. Then you are free to love someone. Without a one-to-one relationship, I am convinced that there is a fullness of life that many frustrated single persons will never realize.

Although God may call some people, a very few in number, to stay single, he never intended for there to be so many unmarried people on the face of the earth; this is not in the Scriptures. It is a wrong Pauline interpretation that would suggest that it is always better to be single; this is true only if you are not frustrated or if you are given a special call. No one can do more work for God alone if he or she feels unfulfilled. Most singles I know are dissatisfied and frustrated. A guy walked up to me last week and said, "Where do I fit in? I'm not frustrated with living single." I said, "Great, praise the Lord for it."

There is a philosophy of this age proclaiming that "singleness is great!" Singleness is great only for a certain few people. Christian psychologists boldly claim that to be human is to love and to be loved. Some go so far as to say that the basic

cause of all mental and emotional illness is the inability
to form deep human relationships of love.

When relationships of true intimate love are missing in a
human life it is usually because the person has either selfishly,
fearfully, or timidly kept the door of his heart locked
and barricaded. He is either unwilling to risk transparency, to
expose the most sensitive areas of his soul to another,
or he has tried and has been rejected. It has been stated that the
second hardest, but most wonderful thing in all of the world,
is to engage in the challenging process of living intimately and
growing with another. The hardest thing in all of this world
is to live alone. It is my belief that God intends for most singles to
have what we call the "miracle of intimacy," where someone
seeks their satisfaction, security, and development above their
own and that you in return seek theirs.

There are people who have neglected *loving* the person they
really love—all in the name of a career. We honor many
single professionals. I have heard some missionaries say that they
left their prospective husband or wife on the shores of
America to go be a missionary somewhere. I am not saying they
were not in the will of God. But, I believe that it is a form
of idolatry to put anything before God's priority list of love. Your
career is not the most important thing in your life. I would
give up everything I own and my career, not my ministry, but my
career, if I could have married the person I loved once in
my life. I would!

Careers and *things* are not the substance of life. Next to your
relationships to the Lord Jesus Christ, there is nothing
more important than our relationship to a lifelong partner and to
friends. Yet, we are living in a generation that beckons
and proclaims career and performance over relationships. The
tragedy is that so many of the truths that I am sharing with
you have not come only from singles, but from young married
couples. Even in marriage, when career takes precedence
over relationship, severe problems develop. There is one thing
worse than being single, and that is being married to the
wrong person. I am not putting down singleness; yet I see a

movement today even among churches that says, "Yippee, singleness, successful singularity." Singleness becomes a rally and a liberation movement.

As I have been studying marriages, I find so many times that the very thing that you desire the most is missing even in marriages—the *miracle of intimacy*. The one area of hope in every life is that one can respond to the desire to love and to be loved. We are living in a world that is growing farther and farther away from knowing how to love and be loved. This causes severe problems in friendships and in marriages.

Jesus said if you want to be great, be a servant. I believe a secret to relationships is a servant heart. I know some people who attempt to love but then recoil because they do not know how to be loved, they do not know how to receive. The answer is in the area of priorities, selflessness, and a servant's heart.

I believe that two people can be meant for each other, and because of one's hang-ups or background, the other will have their heart broken. You say, but God will make our marriage happen. I am convinced that there is a point where God does not intervene. I am not saying that God *can't* bring good out of the tragedies of life. But I am convinced many lives face tragedy of heartbreak, not because God did not bring two people together, but because one of those people was not willing to be where he or she should be. I have observed people who prayerfully enter relationships and fall in love and then for some unexplained reason things fall apart. The fact that you enter a relationship hoping God is leading you, does not always ensure that it is going to work out. God will not make that person a robot.

There are four things mentioned by Solomon as means to fullfillment: 1) an awesome reverence for God; 2) a life partner, who mutually gives and receives love; 3) a social life with friends; 4) something with which you can fruitfully endeavor to help fulfill someone else. Solomon says that through all the futility and heartache, strive after these things because they are the gift of God to his people in this world.

Without that key person through whom we gain the strength and encouragement to cope with reality, we try desperately in many unrealistic ways to fulfill our needs. I want to suggest to you that our faith can many times become an unrealistic superspirituality that causes us to escape real life and what God really wants us to do. In other words, you become so heavenly minded, you are no earthly good. In doing so, our efforts range the whole gamut of psychiatric problems from mild anxiety to the complete denial of reality. Our basic need, therefore, is the need to love and be loved and the need to feel that we are worthwhile to ourselves and to others. If some people cannot satisfy their total need for love they will suffer and react with many psychological symptoms from mild discomfort through anxiety and depression to complete withdrawal from the world into a shell. Similarly, but not as dramatically, if we are unable to love we may shun people to avoid the pain of being in contact with those we cannot admit to ourselves that we need because we are afraid of rejection but deep down we really love them. There must always be someone with whom we feel intimately involved.

I suggest to you that one of the first great keys is self-acceptance and that begins by listening to yourself. How many of you really listen to your feelings, probing your thoughts as you think? I mean the *real* you. Jesus said that from the inner-most being comes the real person. Could he be talking about the subconscious, the real you? Could it be that living water will never come from your subconscious, your inner being, until you call a cease-fire between your levels of conscious and subconscious? The only way that will happen is for you and me to accept who we are and love ourselves for who we are. Love yourself and work with who you are. I submit to you that it is a crime to try to fall into any theology that tells you to say you are someone you are not!

Call a cease-fire between your subconscious and your conscious. You will never know who you really are until you start listening to your emotions, your real feelings. It takes time. God will not permit you to fail when you honestly try to see

who you really are. Relationships tell a lot about our feelings.
One of the greatest gauges of ourselves is other people,
especially that group of people we call intimate friends. Everyone
needs someone in whom they can confide. What attitudes
do we manifest in the way we make room for others in our lives?
Our attitudes are revealed as we respond to other people.
The way we deal with others tells us quite clearly our
characteristic ways of dealing with ourselves. If we repress things
in our life, it will show in our life by building a shell and
walls. There will be a superficiality in the way we meet people.
No one will ever be able to get too close to us if there are
things we are afraid of, if we cannot love ourselves. If there are
walls, our fellowship is superficial.

If you have never loved someone to the extent that you seek
their security, satisfaction, and development as much as your
own, you do not know what you are missing. But if you have
ever loved and gone through a broken love relationship, you
understand. I personally believe that if anyone has to go
through life single and not have that fulfillment he will miss the
highest expression of an unconditional servant-heart love
for another person. It is only in that companionship of a marriage
where you are totally able to give yourself physically,
emotionally, spiritually, and mentally to another person
righteously. I believe that God keeps some people single, but I
believe that most are to be married. Perhaps you have
entered into past relationships with hang-ups and smoke screens.
The answer to this problem has to be preventive. There
is a way to look into your life and find out if there are any
hang-ups. Check to see if you are repressing things.

Some of you have just now become secure in your singleness.
I would say to the frustrated single, "Do not be secure in
your singleness." Because there is something better if God will
give it to you. And if God doesn't give it to you, you may
feel somewhat cheated. Do not be angry with God. If you are
frustrated about your singleness, I think the prayer of
your life should be "God, give me the opportunity to be a servant

to somebody that I could love unconditionally. Give me that someone."

As you pray about this matter, keep these four things paramount in your hearts and minds: 1) God is love. God equals love. Therefore, how can you or I have any other priority greater than that? How can you or I ever seek career, how can you or I ever seek fame, success, more than finding relationships of love through friendships and through a life partner and toward God? That has to be our greatest priority because God is love. 2) You are loved unconditionally. Perhaps this concept will change your theology. There have been some people who have been taught that God cannot love them as they are. But God says he loves unconditionally! 3) Jesus is still Lord of history. Jesus is the Lord of history even when it seems as if your world is falling apart. There was a point in my life where I was praising God for some of the most fantastic answers in life. But within a matter of weeks I felt like Job, as news would come from this area: wipeout! News would come from that area: wipeout! News from another area: wipeout! When your world seems to be destroyed, it takes a long time to comprehend spiritually that Jesus is the Lord of life. The providence of God is still at work, so if your world is falling apart I will not simply say, "Have faith, brother or sister." But I will say from the depth of my soul that trusting and obeying God is your only hope and security. 4) Part of our vision as Christians is that you and I are to love God and love friends and love that special life partner. Here is the paradox: I believe if you and I go around seeking to be loved, that is the wrong approach. Instead, we are to seek to love. Jesus said, "He that seeketh to find his life will lose it, but he that loses his life will find it."

Many of you have bypassed relationships that God has meant for you. Perhaps you now stand in greater jeopardy because we have questioned cultural and religious misconceptions. At this point, perhaps you are refusing to accept the sadness in your heart and you are going to dare to take the risk of changing some vision. You are going to be free even if it means some radical changing to adopt some new ideas. Be open to change.

What, then, is an answer for single adults relating to one another, whether frustrated or not, in order to function spiritually and socially in this world? In other words, how can singles love and be loved? Some answers may evolve out of a "family for singles" concept. This concept will provide fellowship for the nonfrustrated single as well as presenting a spiritual atmosphere for the frustrated single to seek a mate. Again, the greatest precaution is: Do not marry until you have found God's person for you!

The "family for singles" concept stresses the unity that exists between a body of believers as members of the family of God. The advantage of this concept is especially workable with single adults. Many are away from parents and close friends for the first time. Aloneness, especially in a metropolitan city, can be a very real problem for many singles. The family concept meets that need for relating and belonging beautifully. A bond develops between the members of a family that gives them a sense of oneness and belonging. It becomes a supportive community of Christians. Jesus inspired this type of family in the Scriptures.

The best prerequisite for beginning a family is to read the book entitled *Body Life* by Ray Stedman. The *Serendipity Series* by Lyman Coleman is a super resource and guide for family activities. How do you locate the family members? Seek out individuals who are "faithful," "available" and "teachable" —FAT. (Use discretion in using that word, *please!*) Ask the Holy Spirit to guide you in the selection of your family members. Sometimes the ones we see the least potential in are the very ones in whose lives God has chosen to do a great work.

The number of family members may vary from eight to twelve. This does not mean that more or less are not right. Some families have gone over twenty and still have been very effective. Because we are dealing with single adults who have been selected through the leadership of the Holy Spirit, the commitment will be lasting and meaningful. With regard to visitors and new members, experience has proven an open concept is beneficial. Many times a new member has brought a new dimension and enthusiasm to a family. Some of your family will leave as God calls them to another geographic location or to minister in another way.

Families may be led by a couple or an individual. The ages may vary. In previous field testing one family consisted of never marrieds, divorcees, widows, and widowers. Each family member has something unique to contribute—just as our natural family members do—and variety can be exciting and add a healthy dimension. You may meet in an apartment or home. You may want to meet at the same place each week or at the different members' homes.

The suggested format may vary to meet the needs of each family. Some general guidelines are presented in the following:

Agape Meal. Many of the groups eat together in what we call an agape meal. This may be a "brown bag" event or a full meal. It can be a covered dish or one person may prepare the meal and the others may pay a specified amount to cover the cost. The time the family meets will influence this aspect of the format.

You may choose to not have a meal. However, you will notice that Jesus often used mealtime with his people. There is a natural relaxation and comfortable atmosphere set by eating together, so bear in mind this can be a definite asset to your family.

Sharing. The next step is a share time. Members of the family are asked to share with the group what has happened to them that week in their Christian walk. They share victories, defeats, needs, and prayer requests. This is a very valuable time, as the family members begin to open up to each other. However, one thing should be mentioned: leader, beware that the members do not ramble and that any one person does not monopolize the time.

Conversational Prayer. The next part of the get-together is one of the most exciting and edifying parts of the family—

conversational prayer. You may be familiar with this concept; if not, it is suggested you read Rosalind Rinker's book, *Prayer! Conversing with God.* Conversational prayer is, by definition, conversational. It is geared to allow a free-flowing leadership of the Holy Spirit.

How do we carry on a conversation with each other? One person speaks, another comments, the topic changes. This is the way conversational prayer works. One prays about things as God brings them to mind, and not every one is led to pray about the same thing. There should be no fear of silences; sometimes this is when the Spirit is most evidently at work. As the leader, be sure the prayer time is opened by one whose very conversation with God is expectant. This may affect the whole prayer time. Close the prayer time yourself or choose someone you have confidence will close when he or she feels the leadership of the Holy Spirit.

Many times as prayers are voiced, another member will claim a promise from God's Word for that prayer. Scriptural exhortation is a very beautiful by-product of conversational prayer.

Memorization. Scripture memory is encouraged at the discretion of the leader to be related to the problems of the week. It may be a specific assigned Scripture or be chosen by an individual. For instance, it could be a verse that someone learned experimentally that week.

Bible Study. Bible study is a vital part of the family. It should be the aim of the leader to allow the family members to gradually do more of the teaching. This is accomplished by giving in advance assignments, memory work, and projects to certain individuals. As the family progresses, the ratio of leader/member participation should change, resulting in the leader doing 30 percent of the teaching and the group responding with 70 percent. This is gradual and the percentage depends on the individual group. If we are to develop mature Christians, our goal should be to see the family members take more responsibility and develop in their study abilities, resulting in the growth of the family of God, and greater spirit of unity.

Interaction Session. This last phase of the family meeting, which is called an interaction time, requires the discernment of the leader to know when the timing is right. The basic purpose is to allow individuals the opportunity to be affirmed and to be able to interact and get acquainted on a smaller group level. The whole strategy of the interaction session is to divide your group into smaller multiple groups whenever possible. A group of twelve could be divided into multiples of two, three, or four persons to a group. After awhile, these sessions are spontaneous.

A word of encouragement before you venture into this concept. Creativity and freedom are important words to remember with the family. The format, fellowships, etc., set forth in this chapter may not always be the best for your family. It has proven successful for many, as have variations. As the leader, seek to be sensitive to the leadership of the Holy Spirit: "...where the Spirit of the Lord is, there is liberty" (2 Corinthians 3:17, NASB). Do not be afraid to be creative in your disciple training; remember that creativity is the Holy Spirit at work in *you!* Establish in your own mind a blueprint for your group. Meeting the needs of your family to develop them as mature people may mean concentration in different areas of need.

There will come a time when you feel the Holy Spirit has truly made you a "family." This is an exciting time and creates a new freedom and openness in the family as the members begin to trust, depend on, and edify each other.

The family concept may be one of the most effective ways of meeting the needs of many frustrated singles as they seek a mate. At the same time, it will minister to the fellowship needs of the nonfrustrated single adult.

Melva Cook
Church Program Consultant
Sunday School Board
Southern Baptist Convention
Nashville, Tennessee

7

ONE STEP AT A TIME

"The question of whom a person chooses to marry must be related to the question of when a person becomes ready to marry, for when conscious and unconscious preparation for marriage has been completed the proper person often mysteriously appears."[1]

If Theodore Lidz is right, then I never did complete my conscious and unconscious preparation for marriage, because the right person never did appear. There have been near misses, but each time either he or I (or both) decided against it. Am I afraid of marriage for some reason? Am I more interested in a career? Am I too self-centered? Do I take "fairy tales" too seriously, leading me to believe that a knight in shining armor, mounted on a white horse, will come along if I wait? I honestly do not know. "The life development of many persons does not lead to the potentiality of further growth through marriage or for the assumption of the intimate relatedness and the responsibilities of parenthood. Many such persons correctly realize that their future will be more secure and complete if it is pursued in some other direction."[2] Maybe I fall in that category—but, if I do, it is on the subconscious level.

There never was a time when I felt God was calling me to a life of singlehood (or to a life of marriage either, for that matter). Nor did I ever consciously decide I did not want to get married. It just happened. Or it did not happen, depending on which way you look at it. I do not dislike men; some of my best friends are men!

In my childhood, little girls played mother and wife and expected to grow up into these roles. I mothered dozens of dolls and developed my own recipe for chinaberry mud pies. I knew women who were not domestic; however, some of them were very special to me. There were the two daughters of neighbors who worked in mysterious places called offices and wore the most glamorous clothes I had seen in all my fourteen or fifteen years. Some of those clothes even got handed down to me—utter bliss! I thought working in an office was the height of sophistication. Subconsciously, I may have wanted a life like this, but I doubt it. My little-girl play was centered around homemaking rather than career. I can not recall teenage daydreaming about anything but getting married and living happily ever after.

Struggle is a popular word now, but not one I would use in describing my life. As I think back now, things seem to have been relatively easy for me.

The summer before my senior year at college, I went with two friends for a hike up Kitazuma at Ridgecrest, the Baptist Conference Center in North Carolina. We separated near the top of the mountain and each of us selected a spot for a quiet time alone.

I was concerned because I had received no "heavenly vision" concerning my plans after college. I intended to enter seminary, but I wanted a "one-two-three plan" for life. As I prayed that afternoon, God seemed to speak to me as clearly as he ever had before. "One step at a time," I heard. "Your concern now is in serving your term as BSU president. The next step will be revealed when the time comes." And it has worked that way for me.

I thought I was dedicated to student work, but an article in *The Baptist Student Magazine* created interest in the work of a church secretary—just before a surprise invitation to that

position came from my college church. There, as I worked
with an educational director I became highly motivated in that
area. Sure enough, an invitation came to accept that position
in another church! During my career as an educational
director I received many invitations to "teach study courses,"
often under the sponsorship of the State Sunday School
Department. That resulted in my going there as an associate.

Feeling the need of more practical church experience
later, I took more seminary work and then went to a church (and
later another) as a director of children's work. The next
step was the Sunday School Board of the Southern Baptist
Convention.

Here I was involved in editorial work for six years, but it did
not take six years for me to realize I was ready for change.
Editorial work became too routine for me. However, understanding supervisors gave me opportunity to break the
monotony by doing field work (more than half my time one year)
and then a half-time special assignment in long-range planning.

As a result of that assignment, I became a staff consultant
to the department management, with responsibilities in
long-range planning, program design, and research. I was the
first and, at that time, the only woman in such a position
at the Board, which is probably a little unusual since I have never
been a "women's libber."

When reorganization eliminated all staff consultants in
long-range planning and thus left me on the payroll but without
a job, I considered leaving the Sunday School Board. Pulling
up roots after thirteen years is not easy, however, so I took
a position even though it held little appeal for me. Was I
right in taking it? I do not know. It was a job with more
status than my previous one, but with the same job rating and
same salary. It was one for which I did not feel qualified
and which I did not enjoy, although I feel that I did a reasonably
acceptable job. Among the fringe benefits was a month's
review and update in systematic theology on a seminary campus,
which I enjoyed immensely.

I often asked myself *why* during that time. Was there

something I needed to learn? Did I need a lesson in humility? Was this all a mistake—either mine or someone else's?

After four years, I felt I could continue no longer and again I considered leaving the Board. Two or three friends persuaded me to ask for a transfer instead. That request resulted (I assume) in my being asked to become a part of the Family Ministry Department when it was organized. Some rather dramatic experiences convinced me that God was leading in this move.

I can look back now and see aspects of that unhappy period which I did not recognize at the time. While doing noncreative work for forty hours a week, I had done my most creative work in my church. I served as chairman of the stewardship committee and I left the median adult (married) women's class I had taught for several years and started working with single young adults. I found the needed outlets for my self-expression. My support systems came from church rather than work friends.

My professional career has been varied—perfect for one easily bored with routine as I am. I have known people who could spend a lifetime happily in the same job. I do not know what influenced me to want to keep moving, but since something has, I am grateful that God has provided the opportunity.

Now what? Am I a church program consultant in Family Ministry until retirement do us part? I do not know, but I am not concerned. I believe God will continue to lead one step at a time.

How about my personal life during these working years? It has always centered around work and church. I have been fortunate in having many friends, both married and single, within a wide age range—both older and younger than I. I have had disappointments in friends. I have been hurt. And I may have disappointed and hurt others. I hope not. Friends have enriched my life, taught me much, and made life a lot more fun.

Writing has been one of my favorite hobbies. Thus, I have written children's books, study course books, curriculum materials, and many articles. I have taken courses in creative

writing and interior decorating, and I read a great deal.
I enjoy lots of things, including travel, music, cooking,
and football. Especially the Dallas Cowboys! My sense of humor
is the quality for which I am most grateful.

How do I feel about my single state? There are things I like
and things I do not like about my life, but I think my
married friends could make the same statement. So that I may
end on a positive note, let me *begin* with enumeration of things
I do not like and finish with a list of things I do like.

I do not like having to find another women to go with me to
places I do not want to go alone. I am more independent
about going alone than most women I know, but I will not go to a
symphony concert or a night movie or a few other places
by myself.

I do not like going from parking lot to the church door (and
vice versa even more so) alone at night. (However, I am
comfortable sitting alone in church; I often would rather sit alone
than with a group of women.)

I do not like caring for a car or putting a ribbon in my
typewriter or assembling any "easy-to-assemble" object, or
anything else mechanical. If I had a husband, maybe he
would assume these responsibilities.

I do not like balancing checkbooks or working on income tax
forms or deciding which is the best investment, the cheapest
refrigerator, or the appropriate insurance policy.
I should have married a CPA!

I do not like having to make all the decisions.

I do not like sexual frustrations.

I do not like not being close to someone.

I do not like not having someone to share my joys and sorrows.

I do not like my nagging fears that I am becoming more
self-centered.

I do not like being sick alone.

I do not like having no one to help with the load when it gets
to be too much for me.

I do not like feeling that some people probably think I could
not get a husband.

And I do not like the prospect of growing old alone.

There are other things I do not like, I suppose, but I will be weeping and wailing if I wallow in the negatives much longer. There *are* positives.

I like feeling that I can cope, and that I can organize my life well enough to avoid chaos. I am not a "Calamity Jane."

I like being alone and quiet when I want to be.

I like being able to eat a bowl of soup, or cheese and crackers and a glass of milk for dinner and then to go to bed at seven o'clock when I have had a miserable day at work.

I like being able to splurge a substantial amount of next week's grocery money on a great pair of shoes, or one more cookbook for my collection, or a maid for a day if I feel the urge, knowing that no one but me will be subjected to a peanut butter diet as a result.

I like being able to make decisions on the spur of the moment without consulting three other people, even though I do not like having to make *all* the decisions.

I like being able to set my own priorities.

I like opportunities to grow, which probably have been open to me more as a single than they would have been had I married.

I like being able to listen to my kind of music, eat my kind of food, decorate in my own taste, and sleep late on Saturday if I desire.

I like not having all the problems of bad marriages that many people today endure. (On the other hand, I like the feeling that I could and would make a good wife.)

I like knowing that I am a whole person in spite of what some say about fulfillment coming only in marriage and parenthood. I think that they don't know what they are talking about!

Do the advantages outweigh the disadvantages? Would I marry now if I had the opportunity? I honestly do not know. My harp is not hanging in a willow tree, however, and I am determined that I am not going to feel or act like a second class citizen just because I am *Miss* instead of *Mrs.*—and I refuse to hide behind *Ms.*

I am not blaming God for my single state. I am not assuming

that he did or did not create anyone for me or that his plan for me is or is not singlehood. Maybe I made the wrong decisions somewhere along the way. Maybe if I had been where and what he wanted me to be, things would have turned out differently. Maybe not. I feel that I am where God wants me right now; I cannot be positive that has always been the case.

I can—and do—enjoy abundant life in Christ. What more could anyone ask?

What are my goals for the future? First of all, I want to be useful in the cause of Christ. That may or may not be achieved through continued work in a denominational agency, but a contribution through my church and through my everyday living is essential.

My second goal concerns personal relationships: I want significant persons in my life—persons whose lives can make a contribution to my life. I want relationships with persons who are as important to me as I am to them, and vice versa.

My third goal: I want to *live* all my life. I hope I will be able to grow until the day I die. I hope and pray that I can have fun and closeness and curiosity and appreciation of beauty and intellectual stimulation and self-respect until the Lord calls me home.

And I hope to hear him say, "Well done."

1. Lidz, Theodore. *The Person*. New York: Basic Books, 1976, p. 422.
2. *Ibid.*, p. 464.

Len Sehested
International Speaker and Lecturer
Fort Worth, Texas

8

INSTANT SINGLENESS: WIDOWHOOD

On a single day in a single hour through a single event I became a single person again. It was a tragic happening to lose my mate in death, yet to waste this experience by not relating my pilgrimage would compound the tragedy. These ideas will expound on the multiple ways of taking a painful, anguishing happening and turning it into victory.

I have read many books on grief because I am interested in better understanding human behavior. In spending time with people who were grieving, I have come to realize that we are all individual in our responses. Due to individuality each person reacts and responds differently to events in life. I am Len, and you are you. You should not try to push me into having the same feelings that you have; nor should I demand that you respond exactly as I do. I hesitate to say what I feel, yet I desire to give hope to people. If a person has not faced grief, then maybe these ideas will better equip him or her to deal with sorrow when it occurs.

I realize that the normal grief process includes an interaction of degrees of shock, panic, weeping, depression, resentment, repression, guilt, physical distress, and finally hope. I did not experience many of the negative emotions. Do not misunderstand; I am not indicating that I am superhuman. In the past, I have had personal experiences that caused me to know that God is present and that he is here to help me in everything that happens. So I knew that he would be with me during my grief process.

I want to treat death as a Christian rather than as a pagan. I have watched people who have attended church regularly, gone to prayer meetings, given their tithes, and done the things that are expected of good Christians. Then, somehow, when death comes, they suddenly become pagan in their responses to death and dying. They act as if God does not exist. As a Christian I feel very deeply, yet my faith in God transcends even my emotions. This is not to indicate that I did not go through stages of grief.

In my pilgrimage through the loss of my husband I went through these areas of grief:

1. Shock. It was a shock that the death actually happened. No one knows exactly how long life will last. I had enjoyed being with and looking after my husband. It was a joy and pleasure to love and live with him. Then the fact that suddenly he was no longer here was very difficult for me to comprehend. I could have gone all my life loving and looking after my husband. When he died, the severance of relationship was a big shock.

2. Disbelief. I had the feeling of unreality. There were times when I realized that I was not accepting his death because I would talk as if he were still here. There was a degree of denial of reality in that I would make choices knowing that "this is what he would like."

3. Loneliness. I missed the companionship, affirmation, and support of my husband. When you love a person, you love the whole person. You love his mind, heart, and everything about him. When all that is suddenly removed, there is a great big void.

I missed him mostly when I went to bed. It was not just sex, it was the total absence of the one I loved. For hours I would just lie there, think, and talk to myself. I still miss the affirmation that my husband gave me. Victor Hugo summed it up best when he stated that we need affirmation more than bread! My husband was a very affirming person. He helped me to do and be more than I thought I could. He was verbally so proud of me. I miss his love, affirmation, support, and gentle touch as well as all his intimacy.

There is a certain loneliness that occurs when your routine is drastically changed. Life is not as "regulated" as it used to be. We always got up at a set time, had meals at set times, went to work at set times, and went to bed at a set time. Now I find that I will have a meal when I feel like it or do what I want to when I want to. Thus, life is not as regulated as it was.

4. Guilt. There are certain areas of guilt that surface. When a person has committed an infraction, he knows it and needs to make it right (1 John 1:9). There is an area of false guilt that plagues people at times. I have had to deal with some false guilt over happenings that really did not ultimately matter. I have false guilt over anything that I desired which would bring an inconvenience to my husband.

5. Acceptance. The major stage of my grief adjustment was acceptance. It is difficult to pinpoint the exact event or day when I realized that I had accepted the death. In some areas of my adjustment, I was slower than in others. It took me about six months really to accept the fact that I no longer had my husband.

I realized that I had adjusted and accepted the death when I finally began to feel that I could do something on my own and function in a way that was good—in other words, when I quit depending entirely on my friends and started making decisions for myself.

In the normal grief process there are some steps or stages that I did not go through. I did not go through negative, heavy emotions of bitterness and resentment. This was so for several reasons. If I did not believe in God, I could ask, "Why did this happen to me?" I could become angry and bitter. But in my daily walk with the Lord, I know that he is real. The Lord does not make mistakes! He is available and adequate for my every need! As far as I know, I am being honest in these statements. I know that God is working in the past, present, and future. I hear people fighting for the inerrancy of the Bible. Yet, I

do not hear anyone fighting for living out the truths that
are expressed in the Bible. I really believe in the Scriptures!

My personal faith pilgrimage reveals a deep trust in God
and his provisions for me. I was unmarried for a long time as a
missionary in India. This brought about a stabilizing
effect on my character in three ways. 1) I knew I was a whole
person. I did not need to have a husband to be a whole
person. 2) I knew that whatever happened, the Lord would
provide for me. 3) I had trusted past difficult areas of my life to
God. Basic is my faith in God and past experiences of his
faithfulness! God is available and adequate for every situation
regardless of how difficult, intricate, or impossible it may seem.

Since the Lord had been good to me in the past, I knew
that he would meet my current needs. This was the stabilizing
force in my grief process. Of course I cried and had my
times of deep grief. There were times when I missed my husband
so intensely! These times came when I wanted to share
with him. It was frustrating to not be able to share as we had in
the past. The tears were very positive as they washed my grief.

Some of the most difficult times in my grief process
had to do with these areas: 1) Sleep. I could not sleep well.
2) Companionship. We were intimate and personal. I could
say anything that I desired. Now I miss that. 3) Togetherness.
We had togetherness. We enjoyed doing so many things
together. We both grew because of each other. We interacted
about everything. 4) Decisions. Decision-making was difficult
for me.

There are specific categories of immediate and ultimate
decisions that have to be made when you lose a spouse. Your
mind, spirit, and body are instantly assaulted by multiple
decisions. Everyone comes toward you from every angle
asking questions. You think, what do I do about this? If I make
a statement, will this be the last word on the issue? Can
I change my mind later? Will I make the wrong decision? I have
never had to think about this type of thing. I prayed that
the Lord would illuminate my mind and my senses as I had
to make choices in these areas:

1. Funeral and burial. I feel that in our society we pay too much attention to all the pomp and circumstance of funerals and burial. As Christians, we need to step back and say, what has happened? One of our loving persons has died. Part of us has died. Yet we know where he has gone. There is no great mystery. We should bury the body in a simple way. The funeral service for my husband was positive as well as a simple expression of his faith. We read his favorite Scriptures and sang favorite songs. We did not want to celebrate death in a pagan fashion. As Christians, we view death as a homegoing and victory celebration. You do not have to "go for broke" one last time trying to tell the deceased that you loved them. Funerals are for the living.

2. Finance. Get a financial advisor who is Christian and credible in knowing how to give quality advice. Most people are faced with decisions of investments, budgets, and estate planning.

3. Remain or relocate. I was faced with the decision as to whether I would remain in the same city or relocate. Since I stayed in the sasme city, there was the decision of whether to sell the house and move to an apartment. I determined not to make any moves for at least three years.

4. Practical matters. There are practical "nitty gritty" everyday things with which we have to deal. Things such as: repairing the house and car, doing the yard, where to continue doing business, and perhaps when to travel.

5. Dealing with children. Since the children were already grown, many matters were already handled. I had to let them know about the death. While they were together we had to decide who would get what as keepsakes were distributed. My children made many decisions easier as they voted among themselves as to who would get what. They were generous with one another. Perhaps one of the most important areas in dealing with the children is to keep in touch with them.

6. Learning to be independent. I did not want to be one of those "clinging widows." I certainly did not want people to say negative things about my dependence on others.

I wanted to be independent, yet I also needed people. So I had to make the decision to be independent.

7. Possible remarriage. One of the things that most people have to decide is whether to remarry. I do not want people to push me into dating nor remarrying. At this point I am not ready to date. When I am ready, I will. I know that I am capable of loving and being loved, yet I do not want to be forced into anything.

There are needs for the immediate as well as ultimate adjusting to the loss of your mate. Some helpful hints for the *immediate* areas are:

1. Express your emotions. You have something very real to cry about. You have lost someone that is worthy and valuable. It is okay to weep.

2. Remember the person for who he or she was. Keep in proper perspective the positive and negative about your spouse. Do not deify nor glorify the deceased. Accept the good and bad as he or she honestly was. As you remember the person you will enjoy putting in practice the good things he or she taught you.

3. Talk and listen. When people want to talk, we must permit them to say anything they desire. Be a "sound post" for the person who has lost a mate. The widow must feel free to talk. As well as this verbal communication, the nonverbal touch and hug is very important to a person.

4. Remind them that God is real. He sees and knows you at this very moment. He has not abdicated his throne. He is with you all the time. He is still who he said he is! God had a Son who died. He knows how you feel. It is hard to think about God in a time of your grief, but he is thinking about you. Romans 8:18-25 proclaims that the present distress is temporary and negligible:

Yet what we suffer now is nothing compared to the glory he will give us later. For all creation is waiting patiently and hopefully for that future day when God will resurrect his children. For on that day thorns and thistles, sin, death, and decay—the things

*that overcame the world against its will at God's command
—will all disappear, and the world around us will share in the
glorious freedom from sin which God's children enjoy. For
we know that even the things of nature, like animals and plants,
suffer in sickness and death as they await this great event.
And even we Christians, although we have the Holy Spirit within
us as a foretaste of future glory, also groan to be released
from pain and suffering. We, too, wait anxiously for that day when
God will give us our full rights as his children, including
the new bodies he has promised us—bodies that will never be sick
again and will never die. We are saved by trusting. And
trusting means looking forward to getting something we don't yet
have—for a man who already has something doesn't need
to hope and trust that he will get it. But if we must keep trusting
God for something that hasn't happened yet, it teaches us to
wait patiently and confidently.* Romans 8:18-25, TLB

There are several areas geared to the *ultimate* adjustment.

1. Love and be loved. Do not wallow in self-pity, because
you will become "hard" and "bitter." No one wants to
love someone like that. Be a loving person. The only way to be
loved is to start loving. It takes a disciplined effort to
start loving. Be a loving person to everyone you meet.

2. Accept events you cannot change. Face reality. Face what
has happened. Your spouse died and there is nothing that
can change that fact. You saw the body in the casket being
lowered into the ground. You know it happened. Admitting the
truth will help you to cope with reality. You cannot bring
him or her back and you cannot change this fact.

3. Build a better self. After all, you are no longer married. The
interaction that you had with your spouse is now terminated.
Relate to yourself and build a better "you." What kind
of person are you going to be now that you are unattached? Are
you going to be half a person? No! You are a whole person!
Is there an area of your personhood that you could not develop
while married? You can work on those areas. There are
several things you may want to do now. My husband did not care

to swim. Now I feel free to swim as well as do some other things that he did not necessarily enjoy. I like going to the beach. Although these are small areas, they are important to me.

4. Care, share, and relate to others. Since I have had the experience of losing a mate through death, I can more clearly identify with people who have lost loved ones.

It is possible for some women to put on the widow's veil and beat their breast with their fists and say, "Woe is me!" But that is not living nor being real. It is better to be with people and interact and learn from them. This dynamic exchange is a giving and receiving which is most meaningful in human relationships. As long as I am sitting at home and feeling sorry for myself, I cannot do anything for anyone. There are some widows who are doing nothing as they wait for the end of life quietly, and so they accomplish nothing. I would rather live "dangerously" in risking my life for others. Perhaps I might not live as long, but my life will have quality!

When I am tempted to give over to the negative emotions of resentment, depression, or despair, I choose to discipline myself to care, share, and relate to other people. There are so many people just shouting to be cared for.

If I could call a meeting of all the widows I would say these things. You were probably honored to have some special guy to love in your life. If it has enriched you, pass it on. If it has not, perhaps you need a new attitude.

Wesley Jackson
Religion Editor
The Times-Picayune
New Orleans, Louisiana

9

LOST AND FOUND, THE SECOND TIME AROUND

The second worst experience in my life occurred in 1976 when my second wife died, some eighteen years after the death of my first wife.

Frances, my first wife, died in 1958 when we were both twenty-six. She was a victim of malignant melanoma, or "black mole cancer." Our daughter, Jacquelyn, was barely four years old, and our son, Charles, was only eight months old. I was with Fran when she died in the hospital after the lengthy illness which had decimated her unmercifully. We had been blissfully married almost five years.

My second wife, Beverly, whom I married in 1960, had been an epileptic since the age of fourteen. We had been married sixteen years when I came home from work one evening and found her sprawled out on the living room floor. This event was not really an unusual circumstance in itself. This time, however, she was already rigid and had turned blue, apparently having suffered a massive heart attack triggered by several successive seizures.

One would think that the second time around the grief and shock would not be as bad as the first time, but it did not work that way for me. Although two different people were involved and a period of some eighteen years had elapsed in the interim, the anguish and heartbreak of losing a mate, and the frustration of impending loneliness were equally excruciating in both cases. Do not misunderstand, I do not mean to be cynical—just realistic!

As a journalist and religion editor for some twenty-five years, I deal almost every day in my life with the hard facts of the relationship of sorrow and faith in God. I can assure everyone that the hard facts about the loss of a mate, be it a husband or wife, young or old, rich or poor, a short or long relationship, with children or without, are approximately the same in any and all cases. It usually appears at first as a helpless, traumatic, and terrifying experience even for most Christians.

As one who deals daily in factual matters, I can also state unequivocally to one and all that there is no "secret formula" or any sure-fire way to immediately alleviate all the trauma. After all, even Christians are subject to normal human behavior. Yet, remember that man-made formulas do not work—God does!

There is no easy way to overcome the loss of a mate—no two instances are exactly alike, as were not those in my own life. But there are warnings about some definite pitfalls that can be passed along to those widowers (or widows) who encounter similar tragedies in their own lives.

I can only make suggestions based on my own experiences; to do otherwise would be mere speculation and, in a sense, a form of hypocrisy. I can relate, however, some of the things I might have done differently had I been more "prepared" (if there is such a thing) for the tragedies as they occurred.

In the first period of widowhood, I was confused, angry at God, the world, heartsick to the point of considering suicide, and mostly feeling very alone and terrified, not unlike a child who gets lost from his parents. I just could not believe this had happened to me—this was something you might read about in paperback novels, or watch, uncomfortably but with immunity, in a tear-jerker motion picture. It was one of those things that just could not happen, not to a young couple in love, certainly not to us. Someone else, maybe, but not to us!

As I began to dwell on this event in the months that followed, "It could not happen to us" soon evolved into "Why me, why me?"

In retrospect, I now believe embracing the "Why me?" attitude is one of the worst mistakes a widower, especially a younger one, can make. It not only fosters a feeling of persecution, along with needless guilt and self-pity, but it also can be the forerunner of a much worse outlook—that of blaming it all on God. This is often followed by a lingering doubt as to whether or not "there really is a God at all." Asking "Why?" destroys the peace that surpasses understanding.

In actuality, this is the time when a surviving spouse needs all the self-confidence, all the moral support, all the bolstering, all the positive outlook, and all the deep-rooted faith in God that can be gained. To remain mad at the world, or at God, is like taking poison to cure an ulcer; it is self-defeating. It can only mire you deeper and deeper in the depths of self-pity. Martyrs have always been in man's midst, but never has there been a significant martyr who was self-made, only a pathetic imitation.

In the two-year interim between the death of my first wife and my subsequent remarriage, I had convinced myself that there could be no other love to replace the one that had been snatched away from me so abruptly. As a consequence, I tried for a year and a half to be as celibate as a cloistered monk. This, too, was a big mistake. I do not advocate that a widower should start "looking around" at the conclusion of a funeral service, but I would say, based upon my own experience, that the intentional substitution of seclusion for companionship in any form only affords that much more time for a person to feel sorry for himself or herself. This is especially true where the death-terminated relationship was a happy one (and I was blessed that I have had two). The "proper" length of time for wearing black mourning attire, of course, depends upon the individual. Alienating one's self from the normal human need and desire for companionship, especially after a "good" marriage, is sheer escapism and running away from reality. In today's vernacular, it is a classic example of "copping out."

There is one unalterable fact that I have learned from two separate periods of being widowed: life goes on—with you or without you. If you are a part of life, it is more bearable; but, if you are not, you could easily be flirting with neurosis, psychosis, a padded cell, or even worse, contemplation of suicide.

When I finally realized that life was still going on and that God is sovereign, I again ventured out into the world and met and married Bev, my second wife. Perhaps it was because we both had had sad experiences, or maybe because we both had been searching for happiness, we were able to overcome our past adversities and had as good a life together as anyone could expect. Because of her affliction, we decided it would be unwise to take on the responsibility of my two children, so when we got married, I decided that it would be best for my children to be adopted by their aunt. I realize now that this was a mistake. I should have been a father to my children.

The main thing Bev and I had was each other and it seemed as though it would last forever, but obviously, it did not. The day I came home from work with a bucket of fried chicken in my hand and found her dead in our apartment was almost as traumatic as the night my first wife died as I sat by her hospital bedside, holding her hand in mine. The emptiness that ensued was almost identical. So, too, was the sudden fear of loneliness, the first thing I felt once the shock of her death had passed. I once again found myself in the unwanted role of the widower.

That was more than three years ago. Despite some later adversity, I have managed to survive. It is true—life does go on!

If you are thinking it has been only "good times" from there on out, you are wrong. Because I had played the celibate monk's role after my first wife died, and because it had been one of the most miserable periods in my entire life, I was determined not to go through "that" again. Instead, I acted impulsively, making an even greater mistake. I decided I would circulate again and even remarry, *as soon as possible!* This "escape" from loneliness turned out to be the most disastrous event in my life. I did this on my own. I had not sought guidance from the Lord God.

Because of the terrible depression I had experienced the first time I was widowed, or more likely, as I have come to realize, because I had been so "settled down" and "so married" the second time around, I was afraid of *not being married*. This is a frightened person's excuse to avoid being "alone." I found myself jumping into yet a third marriage, within less than three months after my second wife had died.

I mistakenly and selfishly found myself too quickly enamored of a woman who had been a close friend to both my late wife and me. It was one of those unfortunate situations where we were both on the "rebound." We had been close confidants to each other through some good and some bad times. At that time, it seemed like the most natural thing for us to get married. We thought this would solve two people's problems in one stroke.

It seemed a good idea, and on the surface it should have worked, but it did not. From this third outing on the sea of matrimony, I learned perhaps one of the harshest lessons of my life. Being alone is not as bad as living with someone you should not be married to in the first place. I can positively say that there is a big difference between being widowed and being divorced; the former leaves far more pleasant memories than the latter.

The widow's and widower's bad memories come about mainly not because of what transpired during the marriage, but rather because of what was not done. One can look back and realize, in retrospect (when it's too late, of course) that: 1) more spiritual time could have been spent together; 2) no relationship should be taken for granted as though it will last forever; and 3) there were always things that could have been done together for which there never seemed to be enough time. This, of course, is known as "hindsight," an indulgence in which we all share.

Currently, I am not seriously considering another marriage, yet I am open to God bringing a special person into my life.

Although I was badly "burned" by the outcome of my latest venture, I nonetheless still am not afraid of marriage per se, albeit I am much older, wiser, and leerier.

One thing which helped me over this last hurdle, which can be applied to widowed persons as well, was participation in a number of church-sponsored seminars for the "suddenly single," where I discovered that there are others with problems as great as mine, if not greater. After having been out of circulation for so long a time, I was one of those fools who erroneously believed that a single, middle-aged man had to consort either with "swinging singles" or make the rounds of the cocktail lounges in order to seek and find female companionship. I was wrong, and I am not at all ashamed to admit it. The church provides an excellent place for fellowship as well as faith.

One positive word of advice, where widowers, widows or the divorced are concerned: one thing which helped me tremendously in my own rehabilitation was a personal retreat I made in the confines of my own apartment for about three days or so, during a week-long vacation. This was a unique, predetermined time of soul-searching for me. Purposely avoiding both other people and a "feeling sorry for myself" attitude, I took the time to analyze my situation. I had a long, and sincere, look at myself during that period, critiquing as best a layman can those things I had done wrong, those things I had done right, what and where I was, and what and where I wanted to be at that stage of my life. Looking at life spiritually and realistically, rather than through either a mourner's veil or rose-colored glasses, I was able to reemerge with a more positive outlook on life, which, after all, will be around long after all of us have been pushing up daisies in a cemetery somewhere. God always works with those who will be totally honest *with him!*

Also, a word of caution is in order. A "personal retreat" of this sort with one's self should not be undertaken too soon after the tragedy. The time is used for sorting out facts, not so you can get away from people. In my own case, I had already been circulating on a very limited basis. I knew that I could be dating some very nice ladies if I so chose, and therefore I was able to undergo this period of self-analysis-in-seclusion not because I was forced to be isolated, but rather because I wanted to. There is an enormous difference between involuntary isolation and self-imposed seclusion, especially when you know that you can "come out of the cocoon" any time you really want to. This makes a vast difference.

As a result of this "spiritual self-searching" experience, I honestly believe I got to know myself for the first time in my entire life. I determined that adversity, be it the death of a loved one or the "bad vibes" after a marriage gone sour, means only a detour on the road to a full and meaningful life.

Another thing I would advise to those who are widowed is that yours is a shoulder either to cry on or to lean upon for those who are novices to the same experience. There is a special group of people here in addition to the churches in New Orleans, where I live, known as the "Comfort Ministry," which is an arm of the Greater New Orleans Federation of Churches. This group is composed of widows and widowers who receive special training and who offer themselves as "listening posts" for the newly bereaved, as well as those who have recently lost a child. While this type of program sometimes stirs up some long-forgotten memories for those of us who are volunteers, it also compensates for itself by affording us the opportunity to help ease the same pain and suffering in the newly widowed that we went through earlier ourselves. The local church is also one of the most meaningful places to seek comfort, adjustment, and companionship.

One reality the widowed person eventually encounters is that those friends and relatives who had given so much consolation in the grieving period immediately following the death of a mate seem to fade out of view after a while. Since the emotion of grief affects each of us differently, there are those who need someone to talk to months, or even years later. Conversely, there are those of us who have been engulfed in sympathy, long after we have decided to proceed with living. Here again, there is no prescribed formula or deadline.

One thing is certain, however, regardless of how many times a person goes through the tragedy of losing a mate, the grief is just as intense each time, as is the ensuing loneliness, desperation, and the anxiety and fear of being alone, which has to be saddest of all feelings in all of mankind. Perhaps my Christian honesty may seem negative and shock you, yet I am being realistic in my faith.

For those of you not widowed yourselves, but who are interested in or know someone who is widowed, this advice is for you: unless a widowed person openly solicits sympathy, do not try to mollycoddle him or her. When they do emerge from their shell, they will need confidence and support—not more sympathy. After all, the widowed person is no less "normal" a person than any other guy or girl; they just have had a different set of circumstances with which to cope.

When the time does come for the end of mourning, the widowed person is really no different than anyone else, especially when it comes to the need to be with fellow human beings.

Segregating the widow or widower from the mainstream of life can only widen the gap which ultimately must be spanned, if a meaningful life is to be lived by that person. The widow or widower finds it an extremely difficult task as it is, without other people undermining the progress that has already been made along the way.

Cliff Allbritton
Editor,
The Christian Single Magazine
Nashville, Tennessee

10
DAWN AFTER
THE DARKNESS OF DIVORCE

Almost every marriage begins in the bright sunshine of happiness, but there are no happy divorces. Marriage, which promised so much in terms of joy and fulfillment in some enigmatic way, somehow went bad and became a dismal, bleak battlefield of unfulfilled hopes, dreams, and expectations.

Even the word "divorce" has a dark connotation—separation, estrangement, and alienation. No sane person goes into marriage with the intention of divorcing. Invariably, when it does happen it comes as an unwelcome, unexpected, and awesome event.

REALITY OF TRAUMA

Regardless of how much some would minimize the effects of divorce, the fact remains that divorce is a devastating blow to the personalities involved, particularly to the children. There may be a certain amount of temporary relief from the nightmarish stresses and struggles of attempting to keep the sinking ship afloat, but the searing pain and trauma flood in like a tidal wave in a hurricane.

Scripture tells us that marriage is the union of two persons into one flesh (Genesis 2:24). This unity encompasses the totality of being—mind, soul, and flesh. Divorce rips asunder and destroys this unity. Much more is involved than two people deciding to go their separate ways. From the personal and divine perspective, divorce is a destructive, cosmic event that touches all of life. Spirits are wounded and crushed almost to the point of death. Flesh is torn apart as if one's body is torn limb from limb. The pain is so excruciating that it is almost unbearable.

The swiftness of the blows and changes which follow are staggering. One day you are at the pinnacle of your career, pastor of a dynamic, fast-growing, exciting church, winning people to faith in Jesus Christ, ministering to those in need, and holding the respect and admiration of church and community at large. Instantly, without asking to know the facts, some people view you as a leprous outcast—an original participant in the unpardonable sin. All the years of training, sacrificial service, commitment to Jesus Christ, and even the call of God become suspect.

Had it not been for the faithful prayers of loyal Christian friends and the Holy Spirit surrounding me as a wall of fire, I would not have made it. In this connection two theological truths should be remembered. First, not all suffering presupposes personal sin (John 9). Second, godliness does not guarantee immunity from suffering (2 Corinthians 11:23-28).

So, there are Christians and Christian ministers who find themselves divorced. They did not plan to be divorced. They did not have a low view of marriage and cop out by not trying hard enough. They are not emotional and moral incompetents. They are average people like everyone else. Their sin is their mistake in the selection of a mate.

Divorce is an unpleasant fact in the real world in which we live. In this situation not only the fabric of the family structure but also the nature and character of the church is being tested. Will the church be authentic? Will the church be true to its best self as the body of Jesus Christ ministering to its own casualties and to the casualties of broken marriages outside the fold?

Divorce is a tragic, devastating dilemma for both the individuals and the church alike. Scripture is unquestionably clear about God's intention for marriage—one man, one woman, united for life (see Matthew 19:6). Yet the wisdom of God has included the provision of divorce for imperfect, sinful mankind (see Deuteronomy 24:1, 3). Divorce is not God's intentional will. It is always less than God's best. The church faces the precarious position of holding up the divine ideals of marriage and, at the same time, attempting to minister to those who have not measured up to the ideals. But the dilemma is not confined to the divorce issue. The problem is far more encompassing—an imperfect church must proclaim a perfect gospel. Those who minister are themselves sinners. We all need grace and forgiveness. The church always has been and always will be one beggar giving another beggar the Bread of Life.

In the real world, the church is called to be more of itself than it has ever been before. She is called upon to minister in the *spirit* of the law rather than by the *letter* of the law. Paul reminded us that "[God] also hath made us able ministers of the new testament; not of the letter, but of the spirit: for the letter killeth, but the spirit giveth life" (2 Corinthians 3:6, KJV).

Thankfully, more and more ministers and church members are seeing the needs of single-again adults and are rising to meet the challenging needs. They are reaching out with love, acceptance, and compassion, following the example of Jesus himself when he was here in the days of his flesh (John 8).

The church that is alive, growing, and ministering cannot and will not neglect the single adults in our land. If they close their eyes to single adults, they close their eyes to one-third of the adult population of the United States. I know of no growing churches that do not have strong ministries to single adults —never-marrieds and formerly marrieds.

Each divorce sounds the death knell for a small civilization. No one involved has to be reminded that a price is going to be paid by each person involved.

Through these black, murky depths of divorce, people by the

thousands wander every day, desperately groping for light and hoping for a better life.

DEAD ENDS TO DIVORCE ADJUSTMENT

Some individuals, particularly Christians, attempt to deny the reality of the divorce. The high ideals of marriage have, rightfully, been instilled into our minds as adolescents. Consequently, very few if any ever expect to experience this stigmatized ordeal. Divorce is simply viewed as an extremely remote possibility—something that happens to others but will never happen to us. Yet it does sometimes happen to us in spite of all our best efforts, and it is hard to accept. Nevertheless, denial and evasion of the reality of divorce does not solve the problem.

Gary, a middle-aged Christian businessman, admitted that he had made mistakes in his marriage and he accepted responsibility for his share of the blame; but he attempted to evade his impending divorce for over a year by means of legal maneuvers in a desperate attempt to keep the inevitable from becoming reality. In the long run, the divorce went through anyway. His inability to face the unpleasant facts of divorce thwarted the healing process of himself, his former spouse, and his children. On the surface, what he did may appear to have been noble, but in reality it may have been an attempt to evade the principle of the cross in the life of the Christian (Luke 14:27).

Betty and her husband were active leaders in their church. Her husband became enamored with other women and divorced her. Yet Betty refused to accept the reality of her divorce. She continued to invite her former husband back into her home on every holiday even though he had moved out and was openly living with another woman. Her excuse for this evasion of reality was, "I want to keep things as they were for the children." Actually, she had not accepted the divorce and secretly hoped that her former husband would return to her.

After a person has done everything that is humanly possible to save the marriage, the healthy approach is to make a clean break with the past and avoid any attempts to hold on to an empty illusion. When the point of no return has been reached, it is totally unrealistic to dream about a reconciliation. If both partners really desire to try again, that is an entirely different matter, but one person trying alone cannot hold a marriage together. When the marriage is dead, the sensible thing is to face the hard facts of reality and move forward.

Another dead-end attempt at adjusting to the trauma of divorce is what I call the "running syndrome." Divorce deals a severe blow to the ego. It causes a person to experience a myriad of doubts about one's self-worth and capabilities to function as a normal human being. In this hectic and scary situation some attempt to bolster their sagging egos through outlandish attempts to prove their lovability by incessantly dating a continuous string of people, one after the other. Inevitably these relationships are shallow and superficial.

Bill made the ego-crushing discovery that his wife was running around on him and having an affair with his boss. His predictable behavior was the same pattern that many others follow. Even though he is a Christian, he continuously dates women on a superficial basis. His faulty reasoning is, "This way I won't have to commit myself and I won't get hurt again." Actually, he insulates himself from the possibility of forming any meaningful relationships in this manner. No, the marathon dating game is not the answer: it is a dead-end street when it comes to divorce recovery.

A third dead-end approach to divorce adjustment is the attempt to "get lost." Former-marrieds by the thousands attempt to assuage the pain of their divorce by a constant frenzy of activity—loud music, liquor, drugs, and multiplied sex ventures. Any temporary relief one might experience by this method is short-lived. Actually, life becomes more complicated and problem-filled as a result of this style of life. Whether we like it or not, the laws of God are inexorable, unchanging, and work with mathematical precision. Those who sow to the flesh reap corruption; those who sow to the Spirit reap life (Galatians 6:8).

In this confusing and frightening darkness of divorce trauma, is there any hope? Are there any answers? The unequivocal word is yes! Into the most dismal and disquieting situation comes the answer of God. "The people that walked in darkness have seen a great light: they that dwell in the land of the shadow of death, upon them hath the light shined" (Isaiah 9:2, KJV).

POSITIVE PATHS TO DIVORCE ADJUSTMENT

If you are a divorced person, you must give yourself time to heal. Try not to become impatient with yourself and your situation. Divorce produces severe grief through which one must work. Even though you might want to "jump over" this part of the process (as one divorcée put it), grief must be fully experienced or healing will not take place.

Authorities in the field of psychology and counseling tell us that there are several definite steps in the process of grief: shock, numbness, vacillation between fantasy and reality, flooding of feelings (depression, loss of meaning, anxiety, hostility, guilt), remembering the good and forgetting the bad, severe, nerve-racking pain, all followed by the pain of loss and loneliness. Finally, there is acceptance and reaffirmation of life. This grueling process requires time, effort, and hard work. In most cases a divorced person should seek out a competent Christian counselor to guide him through these troubled waters.

To enhance the healing process one should seek quiet places. Repeating aloud Scripture passages such as the twenty-third Psalm is very helpful. Picture the healing presence of God as he leads you beside still waters and restores your soul. At this point in time, one should do only that which is necessary. Steer clear of things and places that remind you of the past. Let your mind rest and let God heal your spirit. He truly is the Great Physician.

Healing will be further enhanced by talking quietly with mature Christian friends who understand and who can give emotional support. This will give you an opportunity to drain off the sick and damaged feelings, keep in touch with reality, and enable you to experience a measure of loving concern and acceptance. Be sure that you choose kind, gracious, understanding Christians who can be instruments of the grace of God.

Another positive path to divorce adjustment involves reaching out to people again. After the fiery ordeal of divorce, the natural reaction is to withdraw and live a secluded and reclusive life. After a legitimate healing time, seclusion becomes unhealthy. People need people to maintain sanity and emotional health. One simply must reach out in love to people again. At first, you may be able to reach out only a little bit. But regardless of how raw and burned your feelings are and how frightening and painful it is—one must continue to reach out. Remember, there will be no new life coming to you without the accompanying element of risk.

Christian singles should seek a few mature Christian friends with whom they can develop deep, close, intimate, nonsexual, spiritual friendships. These friends should be carefully chosen because insecurity, fear, selfishness, lack of under-standing, and distrust are constant threats in the context of close relationships. At this point in the recovery process, one should spread his friendships and develop several healthy, wholesome, Christian relationships. In order to do this, one must allow his emotional barriers to relax to a healthy level. Vulnerability and risk are necessary or one's relationships will be tragically superficial, wooden, and unfulfilling.

Finding a support group is another positive path to divorce adjustment. Unfortunately this is no easy task. New Testament *koinonia* (fellowship) is not easily found. Many groups erroneously confuse socializing with fellowship. They are not synonymous. *Koinonia* is bearing one another's burdens (Galatians 6:2). New Testament fellowship is getting involved in other peoples lives at the emotional level, not

just the intellectual level. This is whatmodern man is
craving and for the lack of which he is dying. Christians and
churches have much to learn about how to develop and
maintain the loving, caring experience of *koinonia*.

PITFALLS TO PONDER

There are several pitfalls to be avoided on the pathway out
of the darkness of divorce to a life of health and wholeness.
Projection is an ever-present danger. One should avoid projecting
the blame on the former spouse, on parents, and on God.
One lady said: "When God began to unmask my secret desires
and motives, I did what most separated and divorced people
do: I evaded examining my own actions and motives and
focused my attention completely on my former husband's deeds."
Rather than trying to sidestep blame, one must analyze
all the causes for the divorce—physiological, spiritual, and
psychological. Accept responsibility for your share of
the breakup. Remember that not since Adam and Eve has anyone
been completely innocent. In my counseling I have heard
many statements like: "My husband started drinking heavily and
running around with other women" or "My wife became
lazy and wouldn't keep house." These are symptoms, not causes,
of the breakdown of a marriage. The real issue is, Why
did they do these things? What were the underlying causes of the
divorce?

Again, avoid the pitfall of needless guilt by accepting God's
forgiveness and by forgiving yourself. God does not spare
us from the consequences of our deeds, but he does forgive the
guilt of our sin. Forgiveness is the pathway of emotional
and psychic freedom. Bitterness, resentment, and unforgiveness
destroy us. Forgiveness looses us from the chains of darkness
and sets us free. This is what the good news of the gospel
is all about—Christ dying on the cross to forgive us our sins.

Avoid the pitfall of doing rash things to prove your
lovability and self-worth. What we need is the legitimate love,

hope, and acceptance of Christians, not the multiplied problems which casual sex produces.

Avoid the pitfall of getting locked into the solitary confinement of self-pity, bitterness, apathy, cynicism, and unbelief.

There were times in my life when it seemed as if the whole world was filled with total, abject darkness. There was absolutely no light in the tunnel—not even a ray. God did not seem to be alive at all and there was no sign that he was doing anything. Yet somehow I knew that he was there. He was. Finally, when I least expected it, through the fog I saw the light of his plan for me cutting through the darkness.

Avoid the pitfall of rebounding from a bad relationship into a more destructive relationship. Do not allow your feelings of need to drive you into another unhealthy relationship.

POSITIVE POINTERS

As in every situation, while there are some things to be avoided, there are definite actions one should take in adjusting to divorce.

As soon as possible, try to get a handle on reality. Divorce blows a person's mind. The entire range of mental activity is affected. Memory is impaired. Indecisiveness is typical. Thinking is slow, awkward, and inept. The mind has been ripped asunder. Regardless of the effort required, however, try to get a grip on your mind and get your head on straight as soon as possible.

Decide who you are and do not deviate from that identity. If you are a Christian you are the same person you have always been, regardless of how others view you. You are a valuable person, a child of the King of all kings, an heir of the kingdom of God. Do not be tempted to change your life-style to conform to the ways of the world just because a divorce has come into your life. Be your own best self regardless of the situation.

Recognize your adversary—Satan. He is at work in our world trying to destroy the effectiveness and witness of the Christian.

Divorce is a crisis situation in which Satan has an unfair advantage. He would like nothing better than to destroy your influence as a Christian.

Learn from your mistakes. Every person makes some mistakes in life. The mistakes we made in the first marriage were usually the result of ignorance. If we repeat the same mistakes in a second marriage we become foolish and the price we pay will be doubly painful.

Realize that you can become a whole person again without remarriage. Many people have the mistaken notion that they need to get married again to solve their problems. They believe that marriage is the only way for them to become whole persons. This is erroneous thinking. To marry under these assumptions multiplies the problems rather than solves them. Jesus Christ was a completely whole person and he was single. He did not have to get married to become healthy and whole. We need to develop into healthy, whole persons first, then we can bring to marriage those capabilities that produce happy, wholesome relationships. Marriage is too demanding a relationship for overburdened or half-persons to sustain.

Learn to laugh at yourself. Life is too important to be taken seriously all the time. We need to be responsible, but humor is healthy (Proverbs 17:22). We are on the road to wholeness and happiness when we can keep ourselves in proper perspective, not take ourselves too seriously, and enjoy a healthy laugh at ourselves.

Commit yourself—your talents, hopes, and dreams for the future—to God through Jesus Christ. Don't try to substitute your plans for God's plans. Do not attempt to become your own god or force your plans on God. One of the saddest statements in the Scripture is: "And he [God] gave them their request; but sent leanness into their soul" (Psalm 106:15). These people insisted on having their own way. God let them have their way. But it was not what they really needed. They received their requests from God, but it did not bring the satisfaction and happiness that they had expected. Be careful how you pray! Be careful what you ask God to give you! You may get it!

Be sure of what you are asking for. Let God choose for you. He knows best. Do not try to rush God. He does not allow us to manipulate him through our prayers. He is God and he knows what he is doing. When you are truly ready to handle a thing or a situation, he will give it to you.

Keep believing that life is worth living. There are times when most of us wonder about the meaning of life and its worth. But deep down inside we know that life was meant to be lived by the challenge and adventure of following the Man from Nazareth. Keep believing in him even when you can't see any evidence of his existence. Remember that he promised, "I will never leave thee, nor forsake thee" (Hebrews 13:5, KJV). He is always with you.

Develop flexible plans and adjust them as God reveals his will to you. Be sensitive to the quiet ways of God's leadership in your life.

Learn to praise God. "Hast thou not known? hast thou not heard, that the everlasting God, the Lord, the Creator of the ends of the earth, fainteth not, neither is weary? there is no searching of his understanding. He giveth power to the faint; and to them that have no might he increaseth strength. Even the youths shall faint and be weary, and the young men shall utterly fall: But they that wait upon the Lord shall renew their strength; they shall mount up with wings as eagles; they shall run, and not be weary; and they shall walk, and not faint" (Isaiah 40:28-31, KJV). This is God's promise to you if you will believe it and accept it.

When divorce occurs in a person's life, he has only one of two options—either to be destroyed or to become a better person. Which will it be for you?

Phylis Campbell Dryden
Working Mother and Free-lance Writer
Defreestville, New York

11

SINGLE PARENT FAMILY

It is often said that when God created the human family, he
ordained that children should have two parents, because
it would be too difficult for one person to raise them alone. Upon
hearing this, married couples usually exchange knowing
glances, for they know how hard it is to survive the challenges
of parenthood.

Ironically, it is the single parent, rearing his or her youngsters
alone because of widowhood, divorce, adoption, or other
circumstances, who is best equipped to understand the value of
the two-parent system. Like the amputee who fully comprehends
the loss of an arm, the single parent can really appreciate
the supremely difficult task of bringing up children alone.

As the single parent of two sons, I actually put myself in double
jeopardy. Following nearly a year of legal separation in
1975, I found it unbearably hard to get by on my own. I opted for
a reconciliation which was to last two years. Finally, after
a total of nearly twelve years of marriage, a divorce changed my
status to that of a single, custodial parent.

The Defrocked Spouse. I can vividly recall my first week as a
defrocked spouse. In any marriage, husband and wife tend to
divide responsibilities, sometimes in a way which conflicts with

established sex roles. In my marriage, I was business manager and financial officer. My husband was the family chauffeur and grocery shopper.

When I took the children to a supermarket on my own for the first time, I was totally unprepared for what was to happen. I walked in and started gathering groceries, bunching them up in my arms as I proceeded from aisle to aisle. I had not even begun to complete my list when both arms were full and I looked like a pregnant woman about to give birth to quintuplet Corn Flakes. Packages bulged out in front of me until they practically fell. Soon the children's arms were full, too. I had not even had the sense to use a grocery cart! Tears welled in my eyes as I thought, "What on earth am I doing? I think I can raise two kids alone, and I don't even know how to shop in a supermarket!" Then suddenly the whole scene looked funny.

Laugh or Cry. It was then that I learned one of a single parent's most valuble resources—the ability to laugh at one's own mistakes! Sometimes laughing at myself has been the only thing to keep me from crying.

In the early days of my divorce, I discovered still more important resources: the strength of God and the power of a spiritual life. I had been married to a preacher's-son-turned-atheist and had gone through an agnostic period myself, but was long since ready to bring my children and myself back to the faith of my childhood. During the foundering marriage, I had been reluctant to make any moves which would cause further division, but once the marriage was over, there was nothing to keep me from pursuing a religious life of some sort.

The Roots of the Church. At first, church was primarily an emotional experience. I sat with my children and just absorbed with all my nerve-endings the peace and comfort of hearing the same "liturgy" I had heard as a child, back when all was safe and sound, and life had seemed to have order and meaning. Many single parents return to the roots of their lives, and divorce opens the door to a church.

I wish that all singles could share my experience. In church, I was surrounded not only by "familiar music" and "liturgical rites," but by contemporary love. People I already respected as private citizens were seated all around me, just radiating charity and kindness.

One Sunday the minister announced a "ladies-only dinner" which would feature a speaker who was a collector of antique dolls. My very masculine son was quite interested in male dolls and I thought he would enjoy the occasion. An inquiry to an older woman met only with shock on her part, so I scrapped the idea. A few days later I got a call from a dear lady who had heard about my predicament through the "grapevine." She wanted to invite my son and me to attend this event. I was very impressed with this Christian lady's hospitality, and I think this incident, more than any other, kept me going to church and searching for a fuller way of life.

Strength from God. Week after week I sat in church with my two sons, ready to give everything up in despair, and silently I sought the strength to get through each new day. Sometimes I felt as if I were holding onto my hope and sanity by a mere silken thread, and the church was my link to eternity. Together, the three of us grew spiritually, and I believe that now our common faith in God is one of the strongest links in a binding family relationship.

Adjustments. At first, however, it was rough. Craig was five when "D-Day" or Divorce-Day came. He had seen little of the good times which his older brother, a nine-year-old, had experienced. Throughout his short lifetime, he had known an atmosphere charged mostly with tension and hostility. A vision of his father wrecking a Christmas tree when Craig was two still preyed on his mind. Yet he was very close to his father, whom he physically resembled. He was fond of me, but not close to me.

Like many other children in the same predicament, he felt that his father had been forcibly ejected into the cold cruel world. He had no comprehension of the many factors which went into this eviction, nor could he be expected to understand that *both* my former husband and I were at fault for our failure to stay together in a peaceful and healthy relationship.

All he knew was that his father was gone, and had left with tears in his eyes. Even though Craig had been shown the spacious apartment in which his dad would be living, he felt that it was not home.

Craig developed serious personality difficulties and began behaving in a bizarre manner which frightened me. After this sweet, lovable child threatened to cut out his cousin's heart, the four of us went as a family for professional counseling.

Craig was a counselor's dream-child. In a childish, yet wholly effective manner, he drew a picture which expressed his feeling about divorce. There were three stick people inside a circle, and one person on the outside.

I felt sure I represented the person on the outside, because I thought the children and their father were ganging up on me to make me look like the bad guy. It did not turn out quite that way. "I'm sad," Craig said, "because Dad's all alone in his apartment, and the three of us are together at home. I just don't think it's fair, that's all."

Recommendations. The counselor made several recommendations. First, he suggested that the children's father and I both make attempts to show them that each of us could live happy and full lives alone. Overnight visits to their father would demonstrate his comfort and well-being, especially if he dated and let the children meet his friends. They could then see that although their father missed them, he was not truly alone.

The counselor further suggested that I stop attempting to simulate family life by still doing things with the four of us together. This was only confusing the children and building up false hopes of reconciliation. He recommended that I pursue a full and happy life of my own, which would include dating.

The counselor assured me that it was normal for children to

resent the custodial parent and to take their frustrations
out on him or her.

I have since observed this to be true even of widowed parents,
for a child may resent the parent who is still living, thinking
to himself, "Why wasn't it Mother who died and left me
instead of Dad?" I have even known children to make life
miserable for the single parent whose spouse has left home to
marry someone else.

Generally speaking, it is the person who shares daily life with a
child who will feel the full brunt of his frustrations as he
learns to live in a one-parent household.

Coping with Authority. For Kirk, my oldest son, one of his biggest
hang-ups has been coping with unilateral authority. He would
much rather play one parent off against the other than
to know absolutely that an order could not be appealed. In a rage,
he once told me that a movie depicting his life would be
called "Uncle Kirk's Cabin," and he took to answering each
command with a belligerent, "Yes, massah."

The matter of discipline has been a third area of growth for me.
I had to adjust to the fact that my household, reduced to
three members, was an independent unit. My ex-husband and I
disagreed on how to run the family. I had to get to the point
where I was not intimidated by him. I learned, the hard
way, to discuss discipinary methods with my ex-husband
privately. I asked him not to challenge or undermine my authority
in front of the children, and I have had to be bold enough
to disagree with him on certain matters and to state this intention
unequivocally to my children.

The children have learned that there are two separate sets of
rules in two separate households—one when they visit
their father and one when they live with me. This is not really a
difficult concept for a child to comprehend. He knows that
he must behave a certain way in school, another way in church,
so why not another way at Mom's, and still another at Dad's?

Disciplinary Problems. Two things I have found unique to the discipline problems of the single parent: first is the fatigue (mental, physical, and emotional) which can render enforcement of rules almost impossible at times; the second is the ensuing need for negotiation. Positive, totally unyielding authority, I have found, is not the answer in a one-parent household.

The double-parent system allows one person to assume the strength which the other cannot not. For example, Mom may have had a tiring day with the children driving her absolutely wild, while Dad can come home and restore order. Or maybe Mom can impart the soothing patience which Dad cannot convey after a frustrating day at the office. Both parents can balance each other, *one taking the role of protecting against the excesses of the other*. But when there is only one parent, and a harried, harassed one at that, who is the buffer? Hence the need for internal negotiation, the frequent need to say, "I was wrong. I became more angry with you than I should have." Also, there may be a need for compromise. In actual practice, some limits may be too rigid or authoritarian.

In the double-parent family, Dad may give in when Mom will not, but the dangers of the single parent are two-fold: giving in too often or too much, or never giving in at all. In the one-parent family, there is no one of equal authority to soften or strengthen decisions. Therefore the limits of discipline may have to be directly negotiated—private to general. It's not an easy task. "Please, please" and pretty blue eyes many times have changed this "general's" orders from no to yes. Other times the rules have had to be tightened because they were too lax. Discipline in the home of the single parent is always in a state of flux, but with love, it can be worked out. There is an important need for constant dialogue within the immediate family: an explanation of motives and a review of an overall plan.

I have set two goals for my children: 1) that they love God with all their hearts and souls, no matter what happens, and 2) that they always be kind to other people. Of course these are the two great commandments which Christ taught, and within this framework, all rules can be explained, even by such simple words as these: "You are not being fair to me by behaving this way. You are supposed to be kind to others, and you are not being nice to *me*."

Too Close. I ran into one danger common to single parents, and that was becoming too close to my children. I found myself confiding dating problems and financial matters to them, both of which were adult burdens to be discussed only with grown-ups. I found that I had to cultivate adult friendships to release this need for meaningful conversation. I also found I had to do this on *my* time, not theirs.

There is not a parent alive who does not know how deeply a child can be jealous of a telephone or how bitterly he can resent its intrusion.

In my case, the problem took on dramatic proportions, when Craig attempted suicide by putting a plastic bag over his head at the age of six. He had a problem and just could not see any way out. I was on the phone and unaware of what was going on. Fortunately, Craig's older brother talked him out of it. I realized how badly Craig needed my attention, and I have since tried to relegate conversations with friends to the after-nine hours of the evening.

Time Out. Another challenge I faced was how to find time to be alone. I am the type of person who needs a certain amount of solitude in which to collect my thoughts and restore my soul. That kind of time is at a premium for a single parent, especially one like me who has to work outside the home.

It seemed to me as if all sorts of demands were being made on my private time. I was either working, driving, or taking care of the children. There was no time to rest or relax, to be truly alone. I therefore set aside an oasis for the soul, one hour a day between the time I got home from work and the time I picked up my children from the babysitter. I found myself in a much better frame of mind to greet them, because I knew the minute they saw me, both children would want my attention. This procedure cut down on the *quantity* of time we spent together, but greatly enhanced its quality. I would highly recommend it for every single parent.

Dating Dilemmas. Dating can be a problem for single parents, especially if the children know that remarriage is the ultimate goal. My children looked upon every man who crossed my threshold as a potential marriage partner, even if this person were merely a repairman or insurance salesman! This could have created embarrassment if I had not turned it into a joke.

The children wanted a man around the house, and their need was legitimate, so I had to accept it. I explained this to my dates, and fortunately they were mature enough to understand when the children asked, "Are you going to marry Mom?"

The man to whom I am now engaged had a perfect way of handling it. He would counter with, "What do you think?" The children would say they did not know, and my fiancé would reply that he did not know, either. This was done in a jovial way which relieved the tension of an embarrassing moment.

At least my children did not follow the example of the daughter of one of my friends, who met her mother's date for the first time and told him, "You're definitely not stepfather material!"

Some children may resent it when their parents start to date, particularly when they are very close to the partner who left home. This is true even when the husband or wife left to pursue another relationship. A friend of mine met strong opposition from her daughters when, a year after her husband left her for another woman, she began to date. She had to be very firm with them, and explain that she had a right to a life of her own, which would include the social companionship of other men. The children saw their mother's dates as rivals for the affection she once held for her former husband, and perhaps they even saw them as personal rivals.

When I first met Mike, my children loved him immediately, but as my fondness for him grew, my youngest son began to get a tiny bit jealous. "Mike! Mike! All you ever talk about is Mike!" Craig blurted out. I explained that my love for

Mike would never interfere in any way with my affection for him
as a son. I tried to lavish attention on the children, so they
would stop viewing Mike as a threat. We both watched, with some
amusement, as the children would make their obvious bids
for my attention, doing things such as trying to sit between us, and
cuddling up close to me at very odd times. They soon
found that I had love enough to share, and they would not be
short-changed in any way.

Who's Who?   Especially if both parents remain in the same
community, it can be very awkward to explain the family
situation to people who do not know there has been a divorce. My
children never seemed to mind this, for they were brought up
to be very frank. "We're dee-vorced," Kirk always tells
people. For some, divorce is seen as a personal failure or
stigma, and these people find it much more difficult to
handle social situations. I think sometimes they communicate
their uneasiness to their children.

A softer sentence, such as, "My husband and I are no longer
together," may suffice, and children can be taught to
say, "Mom and Dad don't live together anymore."

I refer to my former husband as "the children's father" which
identifies my situation to strangers. On a few occasions,
it has been necessary to attend the same function, in which case
I prefer separate seating. In church, one or both of the
children used to sit with their father, while I sat alone. Once, at
a church supper, my ex sat with the three of us. I would
have wished it otherwise, but the bitterness of a divorce did not
displace the need for social amenities, so I stayed where I was.
I was told that I "handled it very well." Only once, at a
Little League game, was there a scene, from which I chose to walk
away.

Flying Colors. My problems as a single head of the household
have been many, and some of them have been serious, but I feel
I have come out of it with flying colors. One of my oldest
son's report cards said, "What a perfect joy! Every teacher should

have at least one Kirk," while Craig's report card describes him as a "happy, well-adjusted little boy."

I believe that there is a special place in heaven for the single parent, and that there are God-given resources to answer every need. All one must do is to seek them out.

David Ring
Evangelist
Kansas City, Missouri

12

FROM CRIPPLE TO CONQUEROR: THE PHYSICALLY HANDICAPPED SINGLE

I am the object of recognition in every crowd of people. Doors are opened at my approach. Others offer to help. Children ask questions such as, "Mommy, what's wrong with that man?" and offer to finish the sentences when I am trying to talk. I was born with cerebral palsy. My physical coordination is affected as well as my speech. Therefore, I have many physical and verbal difficulties.

Perhaps you would consider it most unusual that a man in this condition would be a preacher and evangelist. Although I speak with some hesitancy, people have to listen to me more carefully in order to understand what I am saying. Therefore, I have an advantage over "normal" preachers.

My personal pilgrimage has been one of struggles, heartache, despair, and victory. My father was a Baptist preacher. Therefore, I am a PK—Preacher's Kid. When you are a preacher's kid you go to church whether you want to or not. That means Sunday morning, Sunday night, Wednesday night—every time the doors are opened; good ol' preacher's kids go to church and look like they are enjoying it.

I tell people that I even went to church nine months before I was born. So when you have gone to church as I have, you have been in church! Yet, I thank God for a daddy and mother who took me to Sunday school and church rather than "sending" me.

My homelife was most meaningful in forming my self-awareness and self-acceptance. My parents instilled scriptural principles into my heart and mind. In 1964 my daddy went to be with the Lord. I do not know why God took him, yet I knew by going to church all my life that the Bible said that if you die in the Lord, you are going to be with the Lord and forever be with him. It was a deep comfort to know that "to be absent from the body is to be present with the Lord." Yet, there was a deep sorrow and absence in my life. I thought I needed my dad to help with many difficult physical problems.

I am a "mother's boy." I am not ashamed to admit that fact. I am the baby of eight children. When I came along, all the family members and friends "spoiled me rotten." I will probably be a little spoiled until the day I die, yet I am not sorry for it. I love my family.

One day my mother became extremely ill and had to enter the hospital. In July, 1968, the doctor came to my family and stated, "Your mother will never go home again. She has advanced cancer. She probably has less than six months to live." This news devastated me. Since my daddy had died, I felt that I needed my mother so much more. Now even she would be taken from me.

I did everything that I knew to try to talk God out of letting my mother die. I pleaded with him. I got down on my knees and said, "Please, God, do not take Mother, please." But in October, 1968, God took my mother. I had seen her go from one hundred eighty-five pounds to fifty-seven pounds. This tragedy did something to me. It made me want to die. I was so lonely, I also wanted to die!

Due to the death of both parents, at this time I moved to St. Louis to live with a sister and brother. My life was so difficult. It was not only complicated due to the death of my parents, but also by physical impairments. I said to my sister and brother, "Give up on me, I am a no-good cripple!" Everywhere I went somebody would point a finger at me and say things like, "Look, that boy walks funny. Oh, he talks funny. That boy is not right." My aching heart would break even more as people would make fun of me. It is destroying for a physically handicapped person to be the brunt of laughter or of a joke.

I became more introverted and introspective. Loneliness was compounded by my physical problems. I was tired of living —or really just existing. I wanted to die. Then it would all be over! Most people ignored my real problems and needs. They saw only the speech and coordination problems. Everyone seemed to be giving up on me.

I have one sister who would not give up on me. So I moved to Kansas City to live with her. Thank God for that sister. She took me into her home and really made me part of the family. She believed in me, encouraged me, and loved me. She wanted me to get back in school. My response was, "Why get back in school and be the laughing stock of the student body?" She wanted me to go to church with her. I thought, "Why go to church? God does not love me. If God loved me, why did he let my parents die? Why did he give me a no-good, crippled body?" I was convinced because of these factors that God did not, or could not love me.

One night, in desperation to get my sister "off my back" I consented to go to church with her. It was a traditional church service. I felt extremely negative toward the complete situation. As the preacher stood up to speak, I remember listening and thinking, "I wish you would shut-up. If you will not shut-up, I am going to leave here and never come back again!" Finally the preacher did "shut-up," but the Lord Jesus "spoke-up" to my heart through conviction. For the first time, I realized that Jesus was fulfilling the scriptural truth of Revelation 3:20. My spirit understood that Jesus was knocking at my heart's door and saying that if I would hear his voice and open the door, he would come in and have fellowship with me forever.

That night at the conclusion of the service, I got up and went down to the altar. I got down on my knees and said, "Lord Jesus, here I am. I am a lonely, crippled boy, but if you really love me,

come into my life." It was at that time that Jesus came into
my heart, mind, and life. After this experience, I boldly said,
"Lord, I am a *nobody*, but tonight I want to be a *somebody*."
Hallelujah! That night, April 17, 1970, at 8:45 P.M. I became a
somebody for Jesus.

My complete life-style as well as my attitude changed. I now
have peace, power, and joy! Jesus changed my life. I am
not desperately lonely anymore. I am happy. I do not have deep
sorrow anymore. I have comfort.

Then it was easy to decide to go back to school. Liberty High
School responded to me because I was so changed. School
days were not without difficulty, yet it was a victorious time. The
student body elected me the most popular boy one year.
My class voted me vice-president. The athletic teams elected me
to be the manager for football, basketball, and track. Wow,
what an honor for a guy who is as coordinated as a wet noodle!
I really came to enjoy working with sports. It was fun carrying
water to those dirty football players. I really had a "ball"
in athletics.

In 1971 God called me to preach. One night I was lying in
bed, minding my own business, and God began to convict me that
he wanted me to preach. Instantly, I responded by saying,
"Who, me, Lord? I talk funny—people can't understand me.
I have a physical as well as a speech handicap. Lord, are you
sure you want *me* to preach?" At this point I thought that
the Lord should take a second look at what he was doing. He did
take that second look and still called me! I got up out of
bed and opened my Bible to the Scripture that was burning in my
heart and mind. I turned to Philippians 4:13: "I can do
all things through Christ which strengtheneth me (KJV)."

I determined that I was not going to let a dumb, stupid
handicap stand in the way of obeying the will of God for my life
professionally. So, I have a handicap. What is your problem
today? I am having a fantastic time going all over the country
bragging on Jesus. Cerebral palsy is not going to slow me down!

In 1973 I went into full-time evangelism. I go all over
America telling people that Jesus loves them and will meet their

needs in life. I am deeply fulfilled professionally and personally as an evangelist. In 1976 I graduated from William Jewell College with a B.A. degree. I may be a little slow, since it took me five years to complete the college work. Yet, I am not trapped in society's timetable. In 1978 I was voted to be included in the Outstanding Young Men of America.

One day I will be absent from this crippled body and be present with the Lord. Currently, I do not know what it is like to walk or talk normally. But someday I am going to be in Jesus' presence and look, walk, and talk like him.

Until then, there are several helpful hints that handicapped people should understand and apply:

1) Do not feel negative about your handicaps. Move from self-awareness to self-acceptance. You will not be self-conscious when you put into practice the truth of Psalm 139:

O Lord, you have examined my heart and know everything about me. . . .You made all the delicate, inner parts of my body, and knit them together in my mother's womb. Thank you for making me so wonderfully complex! . . .You were there when I was being formed in utter seclusion! You saw me before I was born and scheduled each day of my life before I began to breathe. TLB

2) Do not indulge in self-pity or feel sorry for yourself. If you feel sorry for yourself, then others will smother you with "sloppy" pity. Some handicapped people need to understand that negative attention is worse than no attention at all. If you feel and act comfortable around people, then they will reciprocate. This will create a pleasant atmosphere.

3) A handicapped person can have a positive, fulfilled life. Remember, people "look and judge" the outside, God judges the inside heart motivation. The truth from 2 Corinthians 1:3, 4 has a deep meaning for me concerning my handicap:

What a wonderful God we have—he is the Father of our Lord Jesus Christ, the source of every mercy, and the one who so wonderfully comforts and strengthens us in our hardships and trials.

And why does he do this? So that when others are troubled, needing our sympathy and encouragement, we can pass on to them this same help and comfort God has given us. TLB

I praise the Lord that I understand human suffering, physical handicaps, and malformations. This equips me to help others to help themselves.

4) Have a proper attitude toward your situation. No amount of psychology or philosophy will change your feelings. The only answer is in releasing your mind and heart to God and asking him to change your heart and attitude. He will complete this work if you will come to him on his terms and do business with him. I am not trying to give you an easy formula. All I know is that when I let Jesus come into my life and be *Lord,* he began to change my heart, mind, and attitudes. The answer is not necessarily in just trying to discipline yourself against poor attitudes, it is in asking Jesus to change your attitudes. In other words, ask him to do for you that which you cannot do for yourself.

If you are handicapped, I desire that these ideas will be made real in your life. Whether you are handicapped or not, I want you to realize that God is using me as a single adult—a cerebral palsied cripple with a speech defect. If God can use me this way, think how he could use you! What is your excuse for not being used more effectively?

CONCLUSION

We are not crusading for some kind of "singlepower." This is not a militant movement for single adults. We are trying to say that for some, singleness is temporary, for others it may be permanent. We will accept marriage if it comes, or singleness if it stays. We have thought of ourselves as persons and of marriage as an opportunity that might or might not come. We are not closed to marriage, yet we are not just flying in a holding pattern, waiting for marriage.

We are not trying to give you a formula for becoming a fulfilled single adult. Man-made formulas do not work—God does! Scripture teaches us not to seek "experiences" but to "seek the Lord." It is God who actualizes the longing soul.

Several of the former-marrieds have revealed that becoming single again was the beginning of a second life and a new identity. It does not matter whether a person is single by having never married, divorced, separated or having lost a mate through death: we have a positive identity. We take our primary identity from Jesus more than from human relationships. Colossians 2:10 proclaims that we are complete in him. Human relationships give secondary identity.

We do not view ourselves necessarily as a single, but as a *person*. Therefore, we have an identity as well as self-respect!

We have sought to refine our character, personality, temperament, and actions into being *whole* persons. Whether we are married or single is not the point. We think of ourselves first as Christians, second as persons, then third as singles. Above all, we have sought to know God—not just to know *about* him but to *know* him personally.

The pattern of our experiences is similar in spiritual and social perspective. We have trusted Jesus Christ as Savior and Lord, yet have journeyed through a trail of tears as we yearned for the scriptural concept of "life more abundant." The details of the writers' experiences are relatively different, yet there is a pattern which emerges. We have gone from self-centeredness and self-effort into dissatisfaction with self, and then moved into an obedience to the Word of God. This has brought about life more abundant!

Scripture boldly proclaims that marriage is good and ordained by God. Yet, Jesus and Paul are major examples of the scriptural concept that it is better for some not to marry. The Bible is tolerant of singleness or marriage. Although the Bible approves singleness, society's disapproval causes the Christian single to be pressured with several issues which are not easily resolved. Society seems to say that marrieds are much more mature. Maturity is a personal thing and marriage is not necessarily a guarantee toward maturity.

In our solo flights, we have learned to distinguish the difference between sensuality of sex and sexuality itself. God has placed limits on genital sexual relations but not on human sexuality. As Christian singles we know that having sexual relations—sex—is not an option. But the problem is that in this society if you are too content with your singleness, some people may think that you are not attracted to the opposite sex. We are sorry for their misjudgment.

Loneliness is an area that we have dealt with in an appropriate manner. Some have realized that the most excruciating kind of loneliness would be the loneliness of a marriage partner. We have overcome great degrees of loneliness through avenues such as: self-giving, work, entertainment, fellowship, travel,

creativity, etc. We have realized that we may be alone in a human sense but not necessarily lonely. Yet, we are not alone!
We know a profound personal relationship with God through Jesus Christ and the peace and power of the Holy Spirit. He does not leave the Christian single alone to cope with singleness. To the proportion that we give ourselves to God, he has the freedom to give himself to us.

We do not blame all our problems on being single. Everyone has areas of unfulfillment, whether married or single.
We have accepted the fact that there is no human who is *totally* actualized. Therefore, there is a realistic perspective concerning human behavior. In one way or another, we have joined Paul in proclaiming: "I am crucified with Christ: nevertheless I live; yet not I, but Christ liveth in me: and the life which I now live in the flesh I live by the faith of the Son of God, who loved me, and gave himself for me (Galatians 2:20, KJV)."

We do not pretend to know all the answers. We only pass on what God has taught us. We desire that God will suit these ideas and answers to your needs.